The Cemetery Fence

By

G. Novitsky

ISBN: 1-4107-4343-8 (e-book)
ISBN: 1-4107-4344-6 (Paperback)

Library of Congress Control Number: 2003092646

This book is printed on acid free paper.

Printed in the United States of America
Bloomington, IN

1stBooks – rev. 06/25/03

Dedication

For Sara

Chapter I.

It's 4pm on a sunny Friday afternoon in a small town sixth grade classroom outside of Detroit Michigan. The bell rings and its time for a weekend of cartoons and bicycle riding for Tommy and me. Tommy is my best friend; he is eleven years old, one year younger than I am. Tommy has light brown hair and he is a little smaller than the other boys his age. I am on my way to Tommy's classroom so we could walk home together like we do everyday. My name is Stephen McMullen. Just like my friend Tommy, I was raised in this small town. We have been friends since our parents introduced us about seven years ago. There's Tommy, as usual the last one to leave the classroom. His teacher Mr.Quinn is holding him up. Mr. Quinn is a heavyset man with some gray in his beard and mustache. He stands about six-foot tall. Mr. Quinn is very mild mannered and pleasant. I'll just stand here by the door and wait for Tommy, as usual.

"Hello young Stephen." Exclaims the voice of Mr. Quinn. "Oh hi Mr. Quinn." I replied, as my voice cracked. "How are you young man?" Mr. Quinn asked. "I am fine Sir, how about yourself?" I replied. "Fine, fine, see that Tommy, you could learn some manners from your friend here. Have a nice weekend boys, I will see you on Monday, and Tommy, on Monday we will finalize our trade arrangements." Mr. Quinn said. "Yes Sir! See you Monday!" Tommy excitedly replied.

I was curious about this trade, but I was not going to push Tommy into details, if he wanted me to know he would volunteer the information. As we walked out of the school gates, Tommy expressed how helpful and caring Mr. Quinn has been. Mr. Quinn has a soft spot in his heart for Tommy. Tommy's Father passed away about a year and a half ago. He was a tall, strong man. He was a policeman who died in the line of duty.

I agreed with what Tommy was saying, then I changed the subject quickly, because I was uncomfortable talking with him about his Dad. I asked him where he wanted to make our Saturday bike ride to. He smiled really big "Lenny's!" he replied. Lenny had the best ice cream by far. Lenny is an older man who we have been getting our ice cream from for as long as we could remember. He had a nice little ice cream shop a couple of blocks from our houses. Once again, I agreed. "Lenny's it is!" I said.

I became uncomfortable when we were about to pass the cemetery where Tommy's Dad is buried. Tommy slowed down, he doesn't usually cry, but I could see tears fighting to come out. I waited until we passed the entire fence before I could come up with something clever to say. I had plenty of time, but it's hard to think during a moment that your friend is expressing his loss for his Dad in his head. We finally passed the fence. "Do you want to have cookies and milk and watch Bugs and Daffy by my house, or by your house?" I asked. I leaned towards Tommy's house when my Dad was home. I just felt funny about him watching my Dad and me together. "Lets go to my house first, Grandpa and Grandma will be there. They are moving in this weekend." Tommy said. "Oh great!" I replied. I love Tommy's Grandparents.

We walked in Tommy's front door. "We're home!" Tommy yelled out. "Hello darlings." Tommy's Mother replied back. Tommy's Mom is a very pretty lady. She is about five foot three with blonde hair. Captain, their puppy came running to us. They named him Captain because Tommy's Father was just promoted to Captain of the police department when they got him. Being a police officer is what took the life of Tommy's Dad. He worked nights, usually until three AM. On the night of his death, Tommy's Mother had gotten a visit from two police officers who informed her that she had just lost her husband to a drug-dealing gangster. Tommy's Dad was shot in the head during a shootout. Tommy's Mom will never forget that night for as long as she lives. She is haunted by it everyday. It also had a very sad effect on Captain. He still hangs around the front door at three AM every morning waiting for Mr. Stages to come in. Tommy's Dad trained Captain. Captain was crazy about him and he still cannot accept the fact that he will never come home again.

"Where's Grandpa and Grandma?" Tommy asked. "Yea, Where's Grandpa and Grandma?" I asked right after him. "Their upstairs fixing up their new kitchen. Go up and say hi. Stevie, I am going to call your Mom to let her know that you are here and staying for dinner." Tommy's Mother replied. "Thanks Mrs. S. What's for dinner?" I asked. "Spinach and liver." She replied. I tried to keep a smile but I just couldn't. "Relax, I gotcha. We're having burgers and tater tots." She said. "Thank you." I said, after a loud sigh of relief. I am not a big fan of spinach or liver and Mrs. Stages knows that.

Tommy and I ran up the stairs to say hi to his Grandparents. Mrs. Stages got on the phone with my Mother; they discussed plans for Tommy's surprise birthday party next weekend at my house. As Tommy reached the top of the stairs, his Grandfather grabbed him and lifted him up. "There's my Grandson." He said, as he lifted him up and down. His Grandpa is short but strong, for a Grandpa. He has short gray hair and a thin mustache. His Grandma came up behind me and gave me a big hug and kiss. "Welcome to our new home little Stevie!" She said. She is also short and a very sweet lady.

We all engaged in that small talk about family and school. Our families have been close for a very long time. After we all had dinner together Tommy and his Grandpa walked me home. It was nice to see Tommy and his Grandpa holding hands and Tommy with a look of security on his face. Tommy needs that companionship again. It's been a long time for him. When we reached my house my parents came out to say hello. They had Tommy's Grandpa come inside for a few minutes to catch up. When they were about to leave I told Tommy to come over first thing in the morning so we could get an early start. We would be putting together some plans for our camp out coming up with some of our friends from school and their older brothers. Then we all said goodnight.

When I went into the living room, my Mother started showing me the supplies for Tommy's party. My Mother also picked up the gift that I couldn't wait to give him; it was a book that he had wanted for weeks. He heard about it from Mr. Quinn and he really wanted to read it. It was about a boy in a similar situation as Tommy who had lost his Father. I made sure with Mr. Quinn that he wasn't going to buy it for him. He was going to, but he said it would mean more coming from me. The book is called "Sudden Track Switch."

I woke up early the next morning, it was about eight o'clock. I had a horrible dream. In the dream my brother Jimmy came to me in a black suit and handed me his bike. "Stevie I am not going to be able to play with you anymore, I have to go on a long trip, far, far away and they say I can't come back and I can't bring my bike. I know how much you love it, so you could keep it." Jimmy said. I started to cry and I tried to scream to tell him to stay, but words would not come out of my mouth. Then he just faded away. "Wake up Stevie!" The voice of Tommy's Father exclaimed. I woke up full of sweat and tears and I ran to Jimmy's room and hugged him. Jimmy pushed me away. "Stop! What the hell are you doing? Buttlump!" Jimmy yelled. "Don't go! You can't leave me! Stay! I love you!" I screamed.

During this our parents came running in. "What happened?" They asked. "I don't know, I guess my personality just won him over after all of these years." Jimmy said. They all had a good laugh and then I told them all about my dream. My dream freaked them out a little too. They said not to worry though; it's only a dream.

About twenty minutes after my dream, the phone rang. My Mother answered it. "Hello." She said. There was a long pause. "No..., no..., no!" My Mother yelled.

Then she got louder, "No ... Please God No...No!" She started to cry. My Father came running in as she hung up the phone. They both went into their bedroom and closed the door. Jimmy and me were very frightened; we didn't know what to do. We went into the living room and discussed the possibilities.

We agreed how happy we were that the four of us were safe in the house. Could something have happened to our Grandparents? Dad's Father and Mother live in New York. We don't see them as much as we would like to, just holidays and stuff like that. Sometimes my parents get worried that they are so far away. Mom's Father and Mother live a couple of towns over from us. We see them at least once a month.

Dad and Mom came out a few minutes later, they insisted that we go back to sleep for a while before breakfast. Jimmy beat them to it; he fell asleep on the couch while we waited for them to come back out.

I went up to my room trying to figure out what could've been so bad that my Mother would cry so much. I tried to forget about it as I was determining how much time would be okay before I went to tell her that I was going to call Tommy to come over. I let an hour pass before I went to her. "Mom, is there anything I could do?" I asked. "No, just be a strong young man and I will talk to you in a little while." She said with tears in her eyes. "Okay, I know your upset right now, but I have to ask you something." I said. "What is it honey?" She replied "Would it be okay if I called Tommy to come over? We are going to ride our bikes to Lenny's for ice cream and plan our camping trip." I said. She began to cry again. "Honey, I have to talk to you." She said. It got real quiet again for a couple of seconds. Tears started to roll down her face. "Stevie, you wont be able to play with Tommy anymore." She said. I froze up and paused. "Its not Jimmy's bike! Its Tommy's bike! Tommy's going away, Tommy's taking the trip far away and not coming back, Tommy's Father told me to wake up because he was taking Tommy away from me." I said. I cried and cried for over two hours with my face in my pillow.

It seemed to me that in my dream, Jimmy was really Tommy and the bike represented how Tommy was taken away. Earlier this morning, Tommy was riding his bike to bring his Grandpa the newspaper. His Grandpa was going to get it himself but Tommy insisted he would get it. Tommy was going to ride to my house but he wanted to get the paper first to show a sign of gratitude towards his Grandpa for moving in with them to fulfill a Father figure roll.

Now his Grandfather cannot get over the guilt he feels about the whole event. Tommy was on his way back, one block away from his house, when a speeding car bounced off a curb and struck him. That newspaper is all that his Grandfather can hold in his arms now. He will regret this moment for the rest of his life. It will take a while before he could hold a normal conversation with anyone.

The whole weekend everyone in my family was trying to do everything they could for me, especially my big Brother Jimmy. He is making plans for us for every weekend for the next six years. Jimmy cares about me very much; he always looks out for my well-being. When we were younger he would always make sure I fell asleep before him, just so he wouldn't worry about me staying up by myself. He also always made sure the bigger kids didn't pick on me. He has always been very protective of me.

The funeral was tough all around, especially for Mrs. Stages. This is her second loss in a year and a half, and they were both sudden. She is planning to go away for a while to try to clear her mind. It would be the best thing for her right now. Her parents planned to stay and look after the house and Captain while she got away. Just getting through the next couple of days was more than enough for her. It is absolute torture. She would lean on anyone that would lend her a shoulder. The people in the neighborhood were more than happy to be there for her.

After a week away from school, which was the saddest and longest week of my life, I was going through my book bag. I noticed one of Tommy's notebooks. I looked through the book and I came to a page titled The Trade, it said...

<u>THE TRADE</u>

I <u>Mr. Quinn</u> agree to be the partner of
<u>Thomas Stages</u> in the Father and son
Homerun Picnic if, <u>Thomas Stages</u> scores an
85% or above on his April 20th Arithmetic exam.

I started to cry again. This was the trade that I didn't want to ask Tommy about. I went to school to see Mr. Quinn. When I walked into his classroom, he was sitting down with his head on his desk. He looked up with his eyes full of tears. "Hello Stevie." He said, and then he paused for a moment. "You know Tommy was my favorite student. I know I am not supposed to share this information with other students, but I just have to tell you, he was my favorite, I loved him. I wont be able to work at this school anymore." Mr. Quinn went on. We got into a conversation about all of the things that made us love Tommy. We laughed and cried for a while before I left. On my way out I looked to Mr. Quinn. "What did Tommy score on the test?" I asked. Mr.Quinn looked into my eyes, holding back his tears. "An eighty six." He said. That was enough for me. I had to stay home for one more day from school. I kept thinking over and over in my head, "An eighty six, Tommy and Mr. Quinn should be partners at that picnic. I decided that I didn't want to be at that picnic now. It just wouldn't feel right to be there.

When I left school, I found myself walking passed that cemetery fence, once again. Only this time Tommy was lying next to his Father. All that went through my mind was, why? Why God? Why? And how we were both together walking passed that cemetery only a week ago. The image of Mr. Quinns face crying went through my head at the same time. I stood staring through the fence for quite a while, before continuing my walk home.

While I was walking I came upon the church; I felt as if something was pulling me toward the inside of the church. I didn't know if it was the wind or if I have some kind of spiritual ability. This could be a possibility since I had that dream at the same time of Tommy's death.

I entered the church and splashed some holy water on my face. That's what I noticed the adults doing the few times I had been in church. My family was not very religious. They figured, since they were good people and they helped out people in need, that would be enough for God to accept them. I stood in front of the candles; I could swear one of them lit up by itself when I looked at them, but that could've been my mind playing tricks on me. There had been so many candles lit, it was probably just my eyes. I just kept seeing poor Mr. Quinn's crying eyes; it was the last picture in my mind.

I kneeled down for a while and just kept asking God why he took my friend away from me. There wasn't an answer. I just figured his Father was getting lonely or there was a Father son picnic in heaven and his Father needed his son. Then I thought to myself how nice that sounded, and that was the story I was sticking with. Maybe I will tell Mrs. Stages that's what happened.

Chapter II.

Tommy's Mother had already began her getaway. It turned out she was staying with some friends in Florida, Mike and Sarah Crawford. They are old friends of our families. Mike is one of the nicest guys around. He would go out of his way to help a perfect stranger, not to mention his own Godson. Mike has a special place in his heart for Tommy. Tommy is his Godson. Mike and Sarah met about five years ago. They fell in love instantly. The last enjoyable time all of our families had together was at their wedding about three years ago. Sarah is a very attractive lady and everyone loved her from the first time that Mike brought her around.

Mrs. Stages doesn't have a full time job in Michigan; she works as a nurse two or three days a week at the hospital. The hospital management is more than happy to let her take some time to deal with her loss. Her job would always be there.

Sarah tried to take Mrs. Stages out to places where she wouldn't think too much about her problems. One night Sarah took her out for dinner. Mrs. Stages spoke about how upset and angry she had been about her husband's murder never being solved and how the murderer is still free. Now she feels the same thing will happen with the driver of the hit and run car that killed her son. Mrs. Stages described her horrific dreams to Sarah, and how she has visions of her husband being shot and her son being hit by a car over and over again.

She also shared how she wakes up in the middle of the night screaming and crying and how she is unable to deal with her pain.

As they were talking and having dinner a heavy set man with an unlit cigar dangling between his thick mustache and beard bumped their table. In a low, solemn voice he apologized, then he complimented Sarah on her pretty smile. After Sarah thanked him, he walked on his way to his table. Mrs. Stages watched him walk away and was very distracted. Sarah asked what was wrong as Mrs. Stages just nodded and commented that the man was just peculiar. They finished their coffee and laughed about the man. Mrs. Stages insisted she was paying the check because of all that Sarah had been doing for her. They paid the check and headed home.

Over the next couple of days, the ladies did pretty much the same things. Mrs. Stages also spent a lot of time walking through the park by herself and visiting some of the sights. She spent some time by the water also. She was happy that she decided to get away for a while.

One evening Mike was closing up at the building where he works security. His replacement Roy had arrived. Roy was a friend of Mike's. "Go home and get some rest, you have a long ride ahead of you tomorrow." Roy said. "You got that right." Mike told him. Mike first went over the details of what Roy had to do on the job, then he said thank you to Roy and told him he would give him a call from Detroit. Mike then headed home.

The next morning Mike was getting some things together for the trip back to Michigan. He was going to be driving Mrs. Stages back home. Mike had also been a long time friend of Mr. Stages. He has been working along with friends of Mr. Stages from the police force on trying to find the killer. Mike was not a police officer; he worked as a security guard and a personal bodyguard. He was good friends with some of the guys from Mr. Stages precinct. These guys have been trying to piece together the murder for over a year now. They didn't have many leads but they were still not about to throw in the towel. Now, not only were they looking for the murderer of Mr. Stages, they were also out to find the driver of the car that killed his son.

Mike wanted Sarah to come for the trip, but she couldn't leave her job at this time. She is a secretary for an attorney in Miami and he is in the middle of some big cases. She said that she would fly up when things slow down. That morning Mrs. Stages and Mike said goodbye to Sarah and headed up to Michigan.

The ride up wasn't as bad as Mike anticipated. He is very emotional about what happened to Tommy, especially since he is Tommy's Godfather. Mike thought Mrs. Stages would be unable to talk or go through the ride without crying all the way up. He also felt she would bring out all of his feelings and it would be too emotional and unhealthy of a ride. It worked out all right; they discussed other things besides the tragedy. They spoke about the old parties and get togethers they all used to enjoy. They shared many great memories. They decided they would all go out for a night or two while he was back in town.

They stopped at a few rest stops along the way for food and a lot of coffee. They even fell asleep at one rest stop for a couple of hours.

The next evening Mike brought Mrs. Stages home and went in to say hello to her parents. Her parents were still very distraught, but everybody just tried not to let all their feelings bring the others down. They were all going to visit the graves tomorrow afternoon. They invited Mike to go with them. He accepted the offer and insisted that he would drive them.

The next day after school I was walking passed the cemetery on my way home. I stopped to look through the fence and I noticed Tommy's Mother, Grandparents, Mike, and a young boy visiting the gravesites. They all looked very sad, except the young boy who waved to me. I wasn't sure who he was, probably one of Tommy's cousins. I just waved back, smiled, and continued on my way.

I returned home and hung around with my Brother Jimmy. We watched some TV and talked for a while about Tommy and what a shame his death was. I told him that the days seem to go on forever without Tommy. I told him how I missed Tommy so much. I noticed that he was becoming uncomfortable because he wasn't sure what he should say. He told me to stay strong, and that he would be there for anything I needed. After a couple of hours I fell asleep on his shoulder.

The next day after school I stopped by Tommy's house to say hello to the family. They were all sitting around the kitchen having coffee. Mike was there too, he was happy to see me. "Hey little guy, you're not so little anymore. Boy, it's been a long time. How have you been?" Mike asked. I told him that I have been okay and that my family and me missed him.

"I saw you guys at the cemetery yesterday." I said. They told me I should have said hello. "I didn't want to disturb you, but I did wave hello to the young boy." I said. They looked at me puzzled. "What young boy?" Mrs. Stages asked. "The young boy standing with you, he was wearing a nice new Detroit Tigers jacket." I said. Mrs. Stages just broke down into tears "Stevie, how could you?" She asked in shock. Then she ran up the stairs. I looked around very confused.

"Stevie, you didn't see Tommy in his coffin at the funeral, right?" Tommy's Grandfather asked. "No sir, I couldn't take seeing that." I said. He then informed me that Tommy was wearing that jacket when he was buried; it was an early birthday gift. There was a gasp and then a silence over the whole kitchen. "There wasn't a boy with you at the cemetery?" I asked. Grandpa nodded, no. After that moment, Mike had taken a special interest in me. Grandpa told me not to worry about Mrs. Stages; he would explain it to her. I thought, that was nice, but who would explain it to me?

I eventually came to the realization that I had seen Tommy that day at the cemetery. It was strange, but it also made me feel good in a way. I felt comforted knowing my friend was still with me.

We all kept that little story to ourselves. We didn't want outsiders to get the impression that I was seeing spirits. The only time it had been mentioned from then on was when I started meeting Mike to discuss my visions and dreams. I told him about the dream I had the morning Tommy was killed. Mike was shocked; we were discussing it over ice cream at Lenny's. This had been the first time I was at Lenny's without Tommy.

Mike asked me if I have had any other dreams. I told him about a dream I had a long time ago, when Tommy's Father was still alive. The dream didn't really relate to anything that was going on at the time, but it just stuck out in my head for some reason.

It started with me walking to school on a very dark morning. Two goolish-looking men were running towards me. The men passed me by, I turned my head and they looked back at me, then they turned around to come after me. There was a bicycle on the side of the road. I got on the bike and started to pedal as fast as I could. I ended up on a road with trees on both sides as far as I could see. It appeared to go on for an eternity. As I was pedaling, I looked over my shoulder and seen the gools in the distance. The gools were riding big black scary bikes and I could tell they were angry. I just kept pedaling faster and faster, as they got closer and closer. I was just about to give up, and then Tommy's Father was running in front of me. He waved to me to turn down an alley. I followed him. He then guided me down the alley. We turned around to watch the gools ride past. We had lost them. Tommy's Father then guided me around corners and up and down corridors. "I will show you it later." He said. "Okay." I replied and I watched him leave. After that I woke up. I don't know what he meant but it still sticks out in my mind.

"Wow, that was some dream!" Mike said as he jotted down some notes, and then he asked if these dreams scare me. I told him that they don't really frighten me; they just make me wonder if they have a meaning. On that note my Dad walked in, he shook Mike's hand and said hello. "Who wants to buy me a vanilla shake?" Dad asked. We laughed as Lenny had Dad's vanilla shake ready and handed it to him. Mike and my Dad sat and talked for a little while to catch up.

I went over to play the video game machine. After Dad and Mike were finished talking, Dad came over and coached me a bit at the game. When the game was over we all walked out together. Dad and me headed back to the house and Mike said goodbye and got into his car and went off to meet with the guys.

Mike arrived at O'Kelly's where he met with some of his police officer friends that worked with Tommy's Father. There is Bob Wilson, Ted Cray, Bill Sullivan, and Vinny Lewis. They all met for drinks. These are the guys that are trying to piece together the murder of Tommy's Father. Now they are together again for another sad occasion.

Bob is a rather large guy; a little over six feet tall, he has dark hair and a dark beard and mustache. He is pretty laid back, and a nice man. Ted is a little older than the rest of the guys. He is a little shorter than Bob. He has light hair with some gray areas. He is as smart as a whip and the other guys look up to him. Bill is another big guy, very muscular. His hair is a little darker than Ted's. Billy loves his beer. He is the first one up for a party. Vinny is a loud mouth wise guy who thinks he knows everything. He is about Five foot eight with dark hair. There is something about him that I didn't like. Maybe its just because he was a little different from the rest. There was also Mr. Glacey, he usually sat in the same corner seat every night, and he stayed until he had to be thrown out. He's not a police officer. He is more like an ornament at the bar.

Bill waved over to Brian the bartender and said it was time for another round. Brian looked over towards Mike "Holy shit, look what happens when nobody watches the door. Anyone could walk in. How ya doing old boy?" Brian asked, with his Irish accent. "I'd be doing a lot better if they could get some descent help in this dump!" Mike replied. "The good help only serve the good tippers!" Brian responded. Everyone around the bar belted out laughs. "So what's it gonna be laddy, the usual?" Brian Asked. "Yea, get him his Shirley Temple, and don't forget the cherry." Ted chimed in. "He may be getting old, but he never forgets the cherry." Vinny said. Another moment of laughter went around. Mike then hugged Brian and asked how business is. "Its steady, Billy boy is keeping the bar in business." Brian replied. Brian and Mike started to make small talk and updated each other on their lives.

Ted motioned to Bob to have a word with him in the back. They grabbed their drinks and moved towards that direction. "What's up?" Bob asked "We are gonna have to stick real close to Mike, he is going through a real tough time. I know we all are, but it's a little worse for Mike, he's trying to put up a front so he doesn't bring us down." Ted replied. "I picked up on that too. We are gonna have to break our asses finding the piece of shit that did this. You know that?" Bob replied "I know, but I don't want you flying off the handle. We need you to keep cool; Vinny's already got me worried. That hot shot has the potential of having the case terminated before it begins. I was talking with the detective on the case, O'Grady. He's telling me they don't have much to go on at the moment, just some blue paint and Firestone tires. We've got to do all we can and stay in constant contact with O'Grady. It's gonna take a while, but it has to be done the right way." Ted said. "I hear you Ted, I would give my house to be part of the team that nails this Son of a bitch." Bob replied. "Lets stay cool, lets make this a nice homecoming for Mikey." Ted Said.

"Excuse me ladies, can I get you's a drink or two? What's the story?" Vinny interrupted on his way back from the mens room. "We were just saying that we gotta show Mikey a good time. Let him take his mind off of this shit that's going on." Bob said. Vinny agreed, "Want me to set him up with a nice broad for the night?" Vinny added. Ted smirked. "How are you going to set someone else up with something you can't find for yourself?" Ted asked. The guys laughed and headed back to the bar.

Back at the bar, the guys had their shot glasses raised in a toast led by Bill. He was just finishing up, "and Florida has one less tired old bastard tonight, here's to Mike!" They all raised their glasses. "To Mike!" "And to the Detroit P.D." Mike added.

G. Novitsky

Chapter III.

When Saturday morning arrived, Mom and I were talking about all of the things that have been going on. I told her that I really haven't been able to get too comfortable at school, although I am trying. She told me that it is only natural, it would take time to get over such a traumatic loss. I told her all about the trade between Mr. Quinn and Tommy. She was moved by the way I came across the notebook. I told her that I put the book away with some of the other things that represent Tommy and when I feel that I need them I look through them.

I also told her that I felt really bad about Mr. Quinn and I was upset that I would probably never see him again. She didn't know that he was leaving the school. She was shocked and thought it was a drastic move but she wasn't going to question how another person grieves. I guess he wasn't setting a good example, running away from a situation. I mean from a teacher's standpoint, he was supposed to be the strong one and the students were supposed to look up to him. I still love him and all, it just didn't seem right. Maybe he would change his mind and come back.

The telephone rang, that sound would now make my stomach nervous. Before my Mother picked it up, she told me that Mr. Quinn would have to do what makes him feel right and I would have to do what makes me feel right. She kissed me on the forehead and told me she loves me. I have been getting a lot of that lately. I liked all of the extra attention, I just wished I could've gotten it under different circumstances.

Mom picked up the phone, it was Mrs. Stages. "Oh, hi, how are you doing?" My Mother said. "So, so." Mrs. Stages replied. She just wanted to thank Mom for all of the family's help and support. She told my Mother how sorry she was for snapping at me the other afternoon. My Mother didn't know what she meant. "I couldn't blame you if you snapped at the Pope, you have more than your share on your plate." Mom said. She also told her if she needs anything at all not to hesitate to call. They made arrangements to meet for coffee one morning when things quiet down. Mrs. Stages told her to make sure she sends me by the house after school one night, as long as I am comfortable with it.

Later that evening I waited for the five o'clock mass to let out so I could have a little time alone in the church. After it cleared out, I went inside. I was starting to like it at church; it was so peaceful and relaxing. I felt like Tommy could hear all of my thoughts from there. I made sure to give him good thoughts. I thought about how everyone was going to get together for his birthday party as I sat down in the back row by the candles. The candles gave me a nice feeling.

I kept my eyes closed and I could feel warmness on my left side as if he was sitting with me. When I started thinking about how we used to meet after school or ride our bikes to Lenny's for ice cream, I could feel him smiling. It was almost like he never left. I told him that I would always be here for him and if there was anything that I could do for him here on earth, I would.

I drifted my thoughts towards my anger of his death for just a moment. The warmness left and a coldness filled my body. I got a little scared and suddenly a hand touched my shoulder. Without opening my eyes I jumped off of the seat and my heart fluttered. I was so afraid to open my eyes, when I did, there was a priest standing behind me. He apologized for frightening me and asked if he could do anything for me. "Not at the moment, but I am sure that I will have some religious questions soon enough." I told him. He introduced himself as Father O'Reilly and he told me his door is always open for when I have any questions of faith. I told him my name and that I would definitely take him up on his offer soon enough. Father O'Reilly gave me a really good feeling, I was happy to have met him.

I left the church at about a quarter to seven and headed home. When I walked into the house there was nobody around. I looked all over the house calling out for Dad, Mom, and Jimmy. I looked out the window into the yard and I saw my Father talking to Mr. Wendell from next door. "Hello Dad, hello Mr. Wendell!" I yelled out. "Hello Stevie!" Dad yelled back "Okay let me go Franklin, I'll talk to you in the morning." My Dad said. "All right boys, have a good night." Mr. Wendell replied.

I asked my Dad where Mom and Jimmy were. He told me that Jimmy is out with his friends from school and Mom is out with Mrs. Stages. I asked how Mrs. Stages was doing. Dad told me that she was coming around; he mentioned what a damn shame the whole situation is. He is just glad that all of us are okay. The whole tragedy made him realize how he appreciates what he has.

Mom took Mrs. Stages out shopping and for something to eat. They went to the mall for a little while and bought some clothes and things. They also stopped in the coffee shop for a cup. They were talking about Mrs. Stages's parents and how nice it was to have them around.

While they were talking a heavyset man with an unlit cigar dangling between his thick mustache and beard was at the counter. He turned around and his elbow hit the counter and his coffee went all over the floor. Mrs. Stages and Mom looked up. Mom let out a small laugh and had to cover her mouth. The man looked over and smiled. "I guess that's why I never made it as a ballerina." He said. Most of the coffee shop laughed, except for Mrs. Stages, she knew she had seen this man before but she couldn't figure out from where.

Mom asked Mrs. Stages if she was okay. "Yes, I'm fine. It's just that man, I know him, or I know someone who looks like him." Mrs. Stages said. Mom gave her a moment to think, "It will come to you when you don't need it to." Mom said. "That's always the case." Mrs. Stages replied. They finished their coffee and left.

Later that night Vinny and Bob were out on patrol. They were discussing ways to catch Tommy's murderer. "I would just love to get my hands on that motherless son of a bitch and beat the living shit out of him with my night stick." Vinny said. Bob told him it sounded like a good idea, but he should cool off while he's driving. A screeching car came around the corner and cut in front of them. "Crazy son of a bitch!" Bob yelled out. Vinny flipped the siren on and floored the ·excelerator. Bob told Vinny not to get too hot. Bob then radioed for backup.

They were on a high-speed chase for a couple of blocks. Bob was on the radio reporting a blue Camaro speeding down Fencin Avenue North. The Camaro side swiped some cars on the right hand side of the road and then swerved to the left and side swiped a tree and stopped. Vinny pulled up next to the car and they both got out with their guns drawn. "Get out of the car! Get out of the car now!" Bob yelled.

Vinny pulled the driver out and threw him on top of the hood as he grabbed his nightstick. One of the back ups grabbed the kid off of the hood just as Vinny slammed his nightstick on the hood right where the kids head was. Vinny and the kid were lucky that the back ups arrived when they did. The kid would've been dead or brain damaged and Vinny would've been in jail. Bob grabbed Vinny to calm him down.

The back ups took the kid into custody and told Vinny after he files his report he should go cool off someplace. One of the other kids leaped from the car and was headed toward Vinny about to swing. The other back up grabbed the kid and hit him and threw him to the ground. He was taken into custody with his friend. The third kid did what the officers told him to do and he was let go after he gave a statement. They made sure his statement didn't include Vinny's temper tantrum. After the paperwork was squared away, Bob and Vinny headed to O'Kelly's; they were meeting Ted and Bill there.

Bob and Vinny made sure to get their story straight, because they could never mention to Ted how Vinny lost control. This was exactly what Ted didn't want to hear.

They walked over to the table where Ted and Bill were sitting. "We're not the guys you're looking for officers, they just went into the ladies room." Bill said. "What's up fellas? I could see you've been through something." Ted said. "We may have met the scumbag that hit Tommy." Vinny said. "Don't bullshit me! What's going on?" Ted leaped up and replied. "Ho, ho, hold up. There is only a slight possibility it could be him, very slim." Bob jumped in to say.

Vinny told the guys what had happened, he left out the part of him almost cracking the kid's head open. Ted was certain that this was a different driver than the one they were looking for, but he told Vinny if he had a strong enough feeling that it was him they would have to look into it. Ted felt they couldn't leave any stone unturned.

Ted made a quick phone call and arranged a meeting with the driver for the next morning. The guard on duty would make sure the driver would stay where he was until then.

The next morning Ted and Vinny met with the driver. They questioned him for quite a while. The kid pretty much had his story together. Ted believed there was no connection to Tommy's death. At the end of their questioning Vinny sort of believed it too. They kept his record in their own separate file just incase. They informed the kid of how bad he screwed up and how he would probably never drive again. They also told him if one of the more experienced judges is on his case, he would be sent away for a few months. They wanted to put a scare into him. Ted and Vinny left together and got ready for their shifts.

Vinny seemed dissatisfied with the outcome. He didn't want to count this guy out completely. He wanted to be the one to nail the driver and the quicker the better. Before Ted left, he told Vinny not to be such a hot head.

G. Novitsky

Chapter IV

Back at school the next day, my Brother Jimmy was eating lunch in the cafeteria with some of his friends. They were talking about the weekend and school things, like cheerleaders and which ones did what. They were in Jr. Highschool. Our schools were in the same building and attached by a shared cafeteria.

While they were eating Jimmy overheard some of the guys at the next table talking. "Ask Jimmy, the freaks brother." One of the guys said. Jimmy got out of his chair and slowly started to walk over to David Stoub. David was the one who made the comment. He is a well know kid in Jimmy's school, very outgoing and usually a nice guy. I don't know why he said something like that.

Jimmy stared directly into his eyes as he headed toward him. David was getting very nervous. David's only strength was his popularity, and after that comment he didn't have much of that. Jimmy with a psychotic look on his face reached to where David was sitting. Jimmy told him to stand up. Jimmy looked into David's frightened eyes and grabbed him by his shirt. "If you are talking about my Brother, your going to have a problem. If I hear anything like that out of your mouth again there is going to be a section of the schoolyard dedicated in your memory. That will be the section that I clean with your remains." Jimmy said as he pushed David back down into his chair and the whole cafeteria stopped to watch.

Jimmy stood in front of David for about ten seconds and then turned away slowly and walked out of the cafeteria to his locker. After he left, the silence broke and everyone was talking about what just happened. Jimmy would never let anyone get away with talking about me like that.

I'm not sure where the comment came from. It could've had to do with my dreams and visions, or my sadness towards the loss of Tommy, or my recent interest in the church, or maybe how I stared through the cemetery fence from time to time. Whatever it was, I was just so happy that Jimmy was my big Brother.

After school Jimmy was walking with a couple of his friends through the schoolyard. They were going to stop for pizza before they went home. David all of a sudden appeared and he walked up to Jimmy. Jimmy's fists clenched as he stared into David's eyes once again. David asked if he could talk to Jimmy for a second. Jimmy's friends backed up and gave them room. "You've got a second." Jimmy said. David trembled. "I'm sorry man. I know your family has been through a lot, and, and, I'm really sorry. That's all. You're a good guy and I was wrong." David said. "Okay." Jimmy replied. "Thanks man, and please tell Steve I'm sorry." David said as he shook Jimmy's hand and ran back toward his friends.

"What a pussy!" One of Jimmy's friends said. "No he's okay." Jimmy replied. The guys then headed to the pizza parlor as Jimmy thought to himself, what an admirable gesture David made.

While those guys were eating pizza and talking about their exciting day, I was at the church. I stopped there on the way home from school. I was talking to

Tommy. It was if he was telling me to go see his Mother some time this week. I tried asking him why, but he wouldn't give me a reason. It was just as if he was telling me that he loved her very much and he wanted me to go to her.

After my discussion with Tommy, I walked back towards the rectory. I was looking for Father O'Reilly. I met another priest and he showed me the way to the priest's offices. I thanked him and then Father O'Reilly seen me and invited me in. I told him he had a nice office and he thanked me. I began informing him of all that had been happening in my life over the last couple of weeks. He spoke to me about it and made me feel very comfortable. He mentioned to me that he heard of situations of people feeling they could communicate with passed loved ones, but he added that my case was extraordinary.

He insisted that I was blessed with a gift and that I should be careful how I use it. I asked him if it was wrong for to me to keep talking to Tommy. He told me to keep talking to him for as long as Tommy listened. He also mentioned that it seemed like Tommy was taken before his time and he may be stuck between worlds. He told me that Tommy might be looking towards me for guidance. I believed him.

I told him that I would provide Tommy with all of the guidance that I could. He told me that he could see that I was a very good friend to Tommy. The whole time that I was talking to Father O'Reilly, I was thinking how interested Mike would be in all of this.

Father O'Reilly told me to continue visiting the church. He said that it is the best guidance that I could offer Tommy. I told him I would most definitely continue; the church had become my second home. I was just about to tell Father O'Reilly about some of my encounters with Tommy's Father. I shut my eyes for just a moment and I seen a drawer slam. It slammed so hard that it startled me. I figured that it was something out there telling me not to bring up my encounters with Mr. Stages. I left on the note that the church had been my second home and I said goodnight.

It was the next morning. Mike had been living above the garage at the Stages's house. He was up there on the phone talking to one of his contacts that gets him work as a personal bodyguard. There had been a job opportunity in the Detroit area. It was to protect a young female singer. She was on tour and she was going to be in Detroit for about a week. The money sounded great. Mike told his contact to sign him up. The job will be starting in a week or two.

Mike would take these types of opportunities when they came up while he was away from his job working security in Florida. He also did this type of work in Florida; he was a bodyguard for a couple of big wigs in business offices in Miami. Occasionally he would get the opportunity to look after some famous people while they were in town.

After he hung up, he made a call to his wife Sarah. Sarah was very excited to hear from him. They told each other how much they missed one another. Mike told her about the job. "Wow, that sounds great. Just keep your hands off of your work!" Sarah said, and they both laughed.

Sarah told Mike that it looked like things at the law firm would be slowing down soon, so she would hopefully be coming up to see him. He was very happy to hear that. Sarah asked how the guys and Mrs. Stages and the families were doing. Mike told her that everyone was doing all right. He also kept her up to speed on the case and the details of his visit so far. Next he started to tell her how very interested he was in the strange things that I have told him about. He mentioned my dreams and told her to keep that between him and her. She was shocked and amazed.

She told Mike that She heard about people with a gift like that. She mentioned that it could be some erie business. Mike added how sometimes that gift was used to solve crimes. He also said that was something he didn't want to push me into, but he would try to get whatever information he could, without pressuring me.

I guess Mike didn't realize that it wouldn't be pressure. I wanted the driver of the car caught also, but I had no idea how I could help.

Sarah told him to be careful and wished him luck. They told each other they would talk tomorrow and that they love each other, then they hung up.

Mike grabbed some of his things and headed out of the door to meet Vinny at the coffee shop. Mike arrived at the coffee shop at around eleven forty five AM. They said they would mcct there at about eleven thirty, Vinny hasn't shown up yet. He was late again. Mike got a coffee and sat down. Vinny walked in at about twelve fifteen and apologized to Mike for being late. "Its okay, its just a good thing I didn't buy you a cup of coffee, it would be warm soda by now." Mike said. Vinny laughed. "Do you remember that kid that Bob and I picked up the other night?" Vinny asked. "Yes." Mike replied. Vinny went on saying how he was convinced at the police station that this kid wasn't the guy they were looking for. He told Mike that he was up all night thinking about it and now he believes this is the guy. He wanted to investigate this kid further.

Mike looked surprised and he told Vinny that he thought he and Ted were sure this wasn't the guy. Mike then asked Vinny if he was going to inform Ted about how he feels now. "I guess I have to, but I would like to see what I could come up with first. Ted needs absolute proof." Vinny replied. Mike told him if he needed help he would be there. Vinny would be going to the station later, he said he would pull the files and attempt to build a case.

Bob walked into the coffee shop and said hello to the guys and got a cup of coffee. Vinny told Mike not to mention what they had been talking about just yet. Bob sat down with them and they discussed the case. Bob mentioned how he was tired of going through every bad neighborhood around talking to gangsters and drug dealers trying to find out who committed a murder over a year and a half ago. "We should just cut our losses, this guy is probably so far away from here or dead by now, we'll never find a trace of him." Vinny said. "I'm not saying we should throw away all of our work, but we have to accomplish something soon." Bob replied "We can't get all negative. We owe it to Jerry to catch this scumbag. (Jerry is Mr. Stages's first name). We made a promise to stick with this case until we close it, and that's what we're going to do." Mike said. Bob and Vinny agreed, even though it was hard to get full agreement from Vinny.

After school that day, Mike picked me up. He told my parents he was meeting me after school. I got in his car and we headed to Vinny's apartment. Vinny was at work. Mike had to stop by to pick up some paperwork. Vinny's apartment was pretty messy and unorganized, but I guess that's the way he's used to it. Mike gave me some chocolate milk and he opened up a beer. "So, what's up? Any exciting dreams?" Mike asked. I started to tell him about my visit with Father O'Reilly when there was a loud knock that came from the back room. Mike got up and walked into that room. He questioned if there was a back door in the apartment. He looked around, but didn't see anything. He came back into the kitchen and said that it was probably the neighbors.

We began talking about the church again. A few minuets later the bathroom door opened and then slammed. Mike jumped out of his seat and ran into the bathroom, all I heard was, "Holy shit!" I ran in with him. It looked as if someone went in there and organized the towels, toothpaste and shampoos on his bathtub floor, and then ran the bath water. We looked at each other puzzled, but what could we do? Neither one of us had every seen anything like this.

We went back into the kitchen and tried to continue our conversation. A couple of minuets passed and then there was another interruption. This time the TV went on and the channels started to change. This was scary. The TV then went off and the light in the bathroom went on. Mike wanted to run out of there.

We calmed down, we both thought it was happening because I was there. The phone rang, Mike picked it up "Hello?" Mike said, in the form of a question, because he thought whoever was on the phone was whatever was in the apartment with us.

Vinny was on the phone; he asked Mike if everything was okay, because Mike didn't sound right. Mike told him he was a little nervous and asked him if there was anything strange about his apartment lately. "Oh, good, so I'm not the only one." Vinny replied "What do you mean?" Mike questioned. "There has been some strange shit going on in that place for the longest time, just recently it has gotten worse. I don't like to be there anymore. I guess I should have mentioned it to you before you went there, but its probably better that you seen it for yourself. That way you'll believe it." Vinny replied. "You bet your ass I believe it!" Mike said.

Mike told Vinny that we were getting the hell out of there. Vinny told him that he doesn't blame us. "Try living there. Boy do I have some stories to share with you. As soon as the lease is up, I'm outta there." Vinny said. They said goodbye and hung up.

We were both relieved that I wasn't the cause of this. Mike started turning off the lights and joked, "It really doesn't make sense, the lights will probably go back on when we leave." He said. We left and Mike drove me home. On the way home I was able to tell Mike about my meeting with Father O'Reilly. Mike joked that we should get Father O'Reilly to come to Vinny's apartment for an exorcism.

When we got to my house Mike came in and sat down with my parents and talked with them for a while. I went upstairs and talked to Jimmy. He was in his room listening to the oldies radio station. He always had that station on. He loves that music. Our

Dad wore off on him. The Doors were playing when I walked in. Even when Jimmy fantasized it was something within reach. Most young guys would picture themselves as Jim Morrison or even Ray Manzarek. Jimmy imagined himself as one of the back ups in the brass section playing the background music to "Touch Me".

I began telling Jimmy about Vinny's apartment. I told him not to tell anyone. He was very interested; he stared at me with his mouth wide open as I told him about what went on over there. I mentioned that Vinny had other stories about it and he was going to tell them to Mike. Jimmy and me were dying to hear all about it, but we knew Vinny wouldn't share them with us.

While Jimmy and me were talking, my Mother and Mike got into a conversation about what they believe is my gift. My Mother doesn't usually bring up stories like these but after all that has been going on she recalled a very interesting moment. She told Mike about a night back when I was about three years old. Dad and Jimmy were sleeping in Jimmy's room. Mom used to use a walkie-talkie, a device that would allow her to stay in her bed downstairs while she listened to me in my crib upstairs.

Mom remembered in detail how she was watching The Johnny Carson Show about to doze off when she started to hear some sounds on the walkie-talkie. She raised the volume a bit. "I heard little Stevie start to cry a little. He started to sound like he was getting comfortable and I began to hear what sounded like a lullaby. It started as a humming and then I began to hear some words. Baby go to sleep. Baby count your sheep. Baby its okay. Baby Jimmy didn't go away. The singing faded away and then I heard a woman's voice say, St. Peters is a very mysterious place. I jumped out of bed and ran up the stairs into Stevie's room and he was sound asleep. I felt a strange presence; I don't know who or what came to visit. I had chills throughout my entire body. I took Stevie back to my bedroom and held him close to me for the night. To this day I believe he has someone watching out for him, someone from the other side. I still get goose bumps when I think of that night." Mom recalled. Mike was shocked and speechless.

Jimmy and me went downstairs for dinner and Mike stayed to eat with us. Nobody at the table mentioned Vinny's apartment. It became a closed subject while we ate. I guess Mike didn't want to talk about it and I certainly wasn't going to bring it up. During dinner my Mother mentioned that she was going to be taking Mrs. Stages to her crisis counseling session tomorrow night. Mom was interested to see what went on there. My Dad commented that it might be good for all of us to hear what they have to say. Mike agreed and told Mom to take notes.

After dinner we all sat around and watched TV. Afterwards Jimmy and me went up to bed. Mike fell asleep on the living room couch. I joked to Jimmy that Mike was afraid to go home and sleep because of what we seen at Vinny's. Jimmy told me that he would be afraid too, if he ever seen anything like that.

Chapter V

Once again after my mind being filled with all sorts of things I fell asleep and got into a really weird dream. It started out that I was stuck outside in the rain and the only dry place that I could go to was Vinny's apartment. I debated whether or not I would go in there, but I was getting soaked, so I had to go in. I walked in and looked around with a very nervous feeling. I went into a dark room in the back of the apartment and I found a filing cabinet. The drawer handle was red hot. I went to pull it open and I burnt my fingers. I tried to pry it open with a butter knife but it just wouldn't open. Someone came up behind me "I already tried, it won't open. I turned around, it was Mike. He looked very upset. He held up a photograph of a wreckage site. It looked like a junkyard; it was a real mess. Mike told me that he left something in the pile of wreckage and he could never get it back. He said goodbye and he got into a train and said he was going to the disaster and he would be back in two months. Then he vanished and the rain suddenly stopped. Then I looked out of the window and I seen my Mom and Mrs. Stages walking down the street with the man from the crisis counseling center. The man and Mrs. Stages were embracing and kissing each other while they walked. My Mother was just looking ahead and walking. I wanted to go out and see her. I ran all around the apartment to get out but the door was gone. I went to go out of the window but the window was gone. I started to cry and I was getting very scared. All of the windows were gone and so was the door. The lights started flashing on and off. A hand came through the ceiling and pulled me out. It was Mr. Stages. He smiled at me and handed me a key and then I woke up. I was full of sweat again. I went to the kitchen to get some water and noticed Mike was still asleep on the couch. I wanted to wake him up and tell him about the dream but I figured it could wait. I just wrote down on a piece of paper, **Don't go to the wreckage.** I put the note in his pocket. This way I wouldn't forget about it. I went back up to bed and fell right to sleep.

The next morning we woke up for school. Mike had already left. Dad said he seen him when he woke up and he told Dad to tell us that he said goodbye. Dad ate his breakfast and told us to be good at school. He kissed Mom goodbye and then went into his car and headed to work.

He arrived at work at about eight o'clock. Dad is an office manager for a banking firm. Everyone in the office likes him a lot. He was walking to his office as he said good morning to all of the people that he passed on his way. He sat behind his desk in his office and opened his newspaper and coffee.

About an hour into the morning his friend Eddie Swanson from the research area knocked on the open door and walked in. Dad and Eddie are pretty close. They have been working together for about six years now. Eddie is a little younger and a little taller than Dad. He is slim and he has blonde hair. Dad and him go to lunch together a couple of times a week and once in a while catch a baseball or hockey game together. "How's it going big guy?" Eddie said. "Hey, not bad. What's new with you?" Dad replied. Eddie told him he was doing okay and he asked about our family. Eddie was concerned about me since the whole Tommy incident. I know Eddie pretty good; he had been over the house a few times. I also went with him and Dad to a couple of games. He's a nice guy; I like him a lot.

Eddie mentioned to Dad that he felt like something strange was going on with the board of directors. He felt a bad vibe coming from them the last week or two. Dad told him that he hasn't heard anything out of the ordinary, but he would look into it. He told Eddie that he was meeting with a few of the guys on Friday, maybe something would be mentioned then. Eddie thanked Dad and headed to his desk to work. Dad shook his head and thought to himself that he hopes nothing is going on at work that is going to affect him or the people in his department. That stayed on his mind for the rest of the day.

Back at Mike's apartment, Mike was up above the garage organizing some of his things; he put his hand in his pocket and pulled out the note that I had left for him. He read it. "Don't go to the wreckage?" he asked. "What does this mean?" He stopped to think. He had no idea what this was. He folded it up and put it in his wallet. He figured it would come to him later. Mike then heard a siren flip on and off, he looked out of the window and seen Vinny in his squad car. Mike opened the window. "C'mon up!" He yelled out.

Vinny got out of the car and headed up the stairs. He greeted Mike. "I think I am on to something." Vinny said. "What do you got?" Mike asked. "That kid

I picked up in the Camaro the other night jumped bail!" Vinny very excitedly replied. "Are you serious?" Mike asked. "Yes, and now he made himself a suspect. I just found out, so do you mind if I call Ted to let him know?" Vinny asked. "Go right ahead, I hope this pans out." Mike replied.

"Hello, Teddy? Vinny asked. "Yea, hey Vin, how's it going? I guess you heard about your little pal jumping bail." Ted replied. "Oh man, you beat me to it. Are you thinking what I'm thinking?" Vinny asked. "Lets say, I'm hoping what you're hoping. It looks like a possibility, but people jump bail all of the time. We've got a couple of the best on it now. His last whereabouts were confirmed to a room above Jays Tavern on Eighth." Ted said. "Wow, you guys are moving quick. Are we going to get a piece of this?" Vinny asked. "Yea, we will be involved once they get a trace on this guy. They were able to pick up on a couple of leads by going through the shit above the tavern. I'll let you know when we are moving in. I want you and Bob there. I will give you a call as soon as I hear something." Ted explained. "Thanks Ted, I'll keep the radio on, talk to you later." Vinny said. "Take it easy Vin." Ted said. They hung up.

Vinny looked at Mike and asked him if he caught all of that. Mike told him he caught enough and asked Vinny if he needed any help with what was going on. Vinny told Mike that he was invited to take a ride to Jay's tavern if he was interested. "Let me get my things. I'll meet you down in the car." Mike replied. Vinny informed Mike of the details on the ride over. They pulled up in front of the tavern and there were two officers guarding the door. Ted was parked across the street. He watched Vinny and Mike walk up to the officers and he just made a disappointing head shake and pulled away.

Vinny and Mike didn't see Ted there. Vinny questioned the officers at the door. They told Vinny that they didn't have much information about the case. They were just there to make sure that nobody trespassed. Vinny got annoyed and he walked back to the car, he has a short temper. 'Thanks for nothing!" Vinny shouted. The officers just nodded. "Thanks guys, don't worry about him, he's having a bad day." Mike told the officers. "Take it easy buddy." One of the officers replied to Mike.

Mike got into the car and told Vinny to relax. "Could this be the wreckage?" Mike thought to himself. "Don't worry, I'm okay. I just feel like this case is being taken away from me. I want to be the one to crack it and I am starting to feel like an outsider." Vinny said. "I'm sure you're not going to be left out. It just seems that you want it so bad, you're letting everything get to you. Now tell me about your apartment." Mike said.

"Oh shit, that's right. Do you want to hear some crazy shit? I came home a couple of weeks ago, really late. I opened a beer and I sat down to see if the news was on. I looked all over for the remote control. I looked on top of the TV twice before I checked the kitchen. I went back in from the kitchen and the remote was on top of the TV, exactly where I looked. Sick shit right? Two days before that, it was sitting in the bathtub on top of a folded towel. Now I don't have a maid and I hardly fold towels, but why the hell would I put the remote in the friggen bathtub?" Vinny went on.

"That's pretty weird, the bathtub was organized the night I was over there too, and with towels. Who puts towels in the bathtub?" Mike asked. "I don't get it either. Another night I was dozing off in my chair and I glanced out the window and something flew by. It wasn't a bird because it sat still for a second or two. I got up to look. I put my head out of the window and looked around. There was nothing. I sat back down and it happened again. I got up again, it was gone again. I sat back down again and of course it happened again. I was pretty freaked out by it, but I wasn't getting up again. Eventually I was able to fall asleep. I have to get out of that place. I find myself sitting staring at the walls waiting to see what's going to happen next. This is really no way for someone to live. It is starting to give me nightmares. What am I supposed to tell the landlord? How is he going to find a sucker to rent that haunted freak show apartment? Are you looking for an apartment?" Vinny joked. "You should charge admission for people to come in, that is one sick place. I never want to go in there again." Mike replied.

They pulled up in front of Mike's place. "I'll tell you some more stories later, I have to go and get Bob now." Vinny said. "Okay, I'll talk to you later on." Mike replied. Vinny pulled away and flipped the siren.

Mike stopped in to say hi to Mrs. Stages before he went up to his place. He usually stopped by Mrs. Stages first to make sure everything was okay by her. Captain ran up to Mike as he walked in. "Hello Cappy, how's it going?" Mike asked the dog. "Hey Karen, what's happening?" He asked Mrs. Stages. (Karen is Mrs. Stage's first name). "Fine, fine, I made some chicken cutlets if you want. They're on the stove."

Mrs. Stages replied. "I don't mind if I do." Mike said as he grabbed some. "Julie will be coming over in a little while. She's going to crisis counseling with me tonight." Mrs. Stages said. (Julie is my Mother's first name). "Oh yea, I remember you mentioning that. That's good for you guys. I hope you get a lot out of it." Mike replied. "I'm sure we will." Mrs. Stages said. "Maybe I'll go with you sometime." Mike said, as he headed to the door. "I'll see you later on Mike." Mrs. Stages said. "Okay dear, you do good tonight, I'll see you later." Mike replied on his way out.

Mom and Mrs. Stages went to the meeting. It was a lot of discussions on how to deal with passing loved ones and what to do in cases of extreme separation trauma and they gave out help line phone numbers. There were also guest speakers. The group told stories about their lost loved ones. Mrs. Stages ended up getting into detail about how she never felt jealousy from her husband. How that was the one quality he lacked. She didn't put him down for it or anything like that. She just let out some feelings that he could've made her feel like he was worried about her meeting other men. This was what these meetings were about. Bringing out all feelings inside.

That was the main thing that Mom recalled Mrs. Stages saying at the meeting. Mom also felt really good about the session. She seemed to have gotten a lot out of it. They shared the details with Dad, Mike, Jimmy and me. Mom told Mrs. Stages she would go back anytime.

The next morning I woke up for breakfast. I went to the front door to bring the newspaper in for Dad. I looked at the front page and I couldn't believe my eyes. I stared at it for about ten minuets with my mouth wide open. This was amazing. The picture of the wreckage from my dream was on the cover of the paper. Every detail was exactly how it looked in my dream. All I could think of was Mike. "Oh my God, could Mike be in this?" I thought as I read the article, it said,

DAMAGED SOUND TRACK

A train en route through Michigan yesterday
Collided with the tour bus of Pop Music Vocalist
Stacey Riches. Riches was coming into Detroit for a week of musical appearances. Four people were killed and at least fifty injured.
Riches is reported to be in critical condition in a coma at a local hospital.
Full coverage on page 4.

As I was telling the family about my dream and how it related to the picture in the paper, the phone rang. It was Mike. My Father spoke to him for a moment and then he told me that Mike wanted to talk to me. Mike asked me if I put that in his pocket. I was confused for a second and then I realized what he meant. "Yes, yes! Don't go to the wreckage!" I said. Mike told me he certainly wouldn't. Then he told me he needed to see me as soon as possible. I told him how great it was to hear his voice and how I feared that he was in that horrible accident. Mike asked to speak to my Dad, so I handed him the phone. Mike wanted to make sure it was okay with Dad that he was going to pick me up after school. Dad told him it would be fine.

When the bell rang and school was over Mike was parked out front. I got into his car and we looked at each other. "Lenny's?" We both said at the same time. On the way over to Lenny's Mike explained to me how he was supposed to be the personal bodyguard for the girl that was now in a coma. I couldn't believe what I was hearing. Now the dream was making more and more sense.

We got our ice cream, sat down and went over the whole dream from beginning to end. We came up with some conclusions. Besides recognizing the relation of Mike to the girl on the bus, we also came to the conclusion that Mrs. Stages kissing the man from the crisis counseling had something to do with Mrs. Stages being bothered about Mr. Stages not ever showing jealousy. We figured that the dream took place in Vinny's apartment because we visited it beforehand. We couldn't figure out what the filing cabinet represented, except that Mike and me were both interested in whatever was inside of it. The two months part was confusing to us. The train made sense, that was obvious. The thing that Mike had left in the wreckage that he could never get back, meant the job he was going to take. As far as the windows and door being gone, we figured that was just something strange that happens in dreams. My Mother being there, we figured was because she took Mrs. Stages to crisis counseling. We wanted to know what Mr. Stages was doing there and what the key he was giving me was for. We figured it meant Mr. Stages had the key to whatever the filing cabinet represented.

Mike thinks that Mr. Stages is sending me messages in my sleep. It sounds bizarre, but it really looks like something like that is happening. Mike told me to bring a flashlight and a pad and pen to bed with me from now on, and as soon as I have dreams like this to write down every detail when I wake up.

Chapter VI

It's Friday morning. I'm in my classroom gazing out of the window. I am pretty laid back. I don't feel like being in school today. I am just waiting for the lunch bell. I just began daydreaming about how a normal Friday at school used to be. I would've been going over in my head all of the things that Tommy and me had planned for the weekend. This weekend I didn't have any plans.

The only thing that I had scheduled was for this afternoon. I was going to be visiting Mrs. Stages. I wanted to see her since Tommy gave me that feeling in the church the other day.

At the same time I was gazing out of the window, my Father was at work preparing for his meeting. He wasn't sure what to expect at this meeting but Eddie gave him an uneasy feeling about it. Dad walked into the conference room with his pad and his coffee and he took a seat by the door. A couple of the guys he worked with were already there. Dad said hello to the guys and they exchanged some small talk as they waited for some others.

The meeting was scheduled to be three members of the board of directors and two other office managers along with my Dad. The other guys walked in and everyone exchanged hellos and good mornings. Everyone was pretty friendly with one another; they had all worked together for a couple of years. There was just one member on the board of directors that

49

nobody cared for too much. They nicknamed him, "Tight-ass". It didn't have to do with his pants, it was that he was extremely cheap and he was always looking to cut costs in places where cuts were not necessary. They never called him that to his face though.

The meeting began; they discussed supplies, profits, and goals for the next quarter. After about an hour of that, Tight-ass announced a problem in the company. He said that after much investigation they discovered an employee who was embezzling money from the company. This grabbed everyone's attention. Tight-ass announced that they were able to pinpoint the guilty party and they will have a follow up meeting once the appropriate action has been taken. "Why does this guy have to talk like this? Just spit it out!" Dad thought to himself.

Tight-ass dismissed the meeting and asked Dad to stick around to have a word. Dad thought to himself how bad this could be. After the room cleared, it was just Tight-ass, another director, and Dad. "I guess this can't be good." Dad said. "I wish it was, I'm sorry it's not." Tight-ass replied. "We need to discuss this embezzling issue with you because, as it turns out the guilty party works in your department." The other director said. He was an okay guy; Dad and him got along well. His nickname was Helmet, which was because of his odd haircut. He didn't know about his nickname either.

"Who is it?" Dad asked. "That's the difficult part, it's Eddie. We know how close you guys are and we really didn't want to have to ask you to fire him. If it's too tough for you, we'll have someone else do it."

50

Helmet replied. Dad stood up "Swanson! No way! No how! It can't be! Not Swanson!" Dad exclaimed. "We can't believe it either. We really wish it didn't happen, but it did." Tight-ass said. "I am going to need a little time to soak all of this in." Dad told them. They understood. "We will call him in and go over the formalities, you won't have to be there if you don't want to be." Helmet said.

Dad thought for a moment, then he told the guys not to worry. He told them that he would handle it. They told him that it had to be done today because of the legal action that had to follow. They asked him if he was sure he could handle it. "I'm positive." Dad replied.

Dad returned to his office and immediately called Eddie in. "Well, your instincts were correct." Dad told Eddie. "What happened?" Eddie replied. "These clowns want to nail you for embezzlement." Dad said. "What the hell? Where the hell does that come from?" Eddie asked with rage in his voice. "I don't know what the hell is going on. I didn't get all of the details. I wanted to see you before I took another step. Could someone here have it in for you?" Dad asked. "Not that I know of, this is pretty screwed up." Eddie replied.

"They want me to fire you. I told them I was going to, but that was only to buy a little time so I could talk to you first. I will go back and tell them that I thought about it and I just can't do it." Dad said. "Thanks, you're a good man. Let them do it. Now I could prepare myself. I am going to need all of the facts from them. I am going to call my lawyer also. I'll leave, but I'm not gonna get screwed for something I didn't do.

These bastards are going to have themselves a really nice lawsuit on their hands." Eddie angrily stated.

"Just stay cool, if we handle this the right way it might be the best thing to ever happen to you. It's not going to be easy to put it together, but it will be worth it." Dad said. "First I am going to call my Brother. He could get me a job at his place for now." Eddie said. "Good, just go to your desk and make your calls and stay cool. I will tell these putzes that they have to fire you. I'll also see what details I could get from them. I'll talk to you later, and we'll get together over the weekend." Dad told Eddie.

Dad waited some time for Eddie to get himself squared away with his Brother and his lawyer. Afterwards he called Helmet to tell him that he couldn't go through with firing Eddie. The only details that Dad could get were, verbal confirmations that Eddie's computer was the one used to allocate funds into an unknown account and receipts that were stamped and signed with Eddie's signature. Dad thought to himself, "Anyone could forge a signature." He thought there had to be more going on with the whole thing.

A couple of hours later, Eddie was working on something with a co-worker named Josh Owens. Josh is a short heavyset man with glasses and dark hair. He's pretty quiet and pretty much gets along with everyone around the office. Eddie was called down to Tight-ass's office while he was sitting with Josh. This is what Eddie had been anticipating. He told Josh he had to go take care of something, and he headed into the office. Eddie didn't raise his voice or make any kind of a scene. He just told Tight-ass that he had the 'wrong guy and that this whole event is far from over. Eddie smiled and walked out. Tight-ass was very nervous about that.

Eddie had already made arrangements with his Brother for a job at the warehouse. It was different work, but it was still descent pay. Tight-ass gave him whatever details he had available. They were awful flimsy. Eddie stopped at his lawyer's office on his way home so his lawyer could get to work on a case right away.

After his lawyer reviewed the details he told Eddie that he has a very good case and they will probably want to settle out of court. Eddie convinced himself that he didn't want to work at that place anymore anyway. He had a clear mind now. He was anxious to start working with his Brother and also getting his lawsuit under way.

School ended for the day and I was just arriving at Mrs. Stages's house. I rang the bell and Captain came running to the door. I walked in. Captain gave me a nice hello, but he walked away very sad as he normally does when he notices that Tommy is not with me. After I heard a crash and the sound of candy falling on the floor, Mrs. Stages walked into the room. She seemed very happy to see me. She had cookies and milk ready for me with Bugs and Daffy on TV. I felt like she really needed me to be there. It was like she waited all week for me to arrive. I guess its because having me around makes her feel like Tommy is not that far away. This is probably the reason Tommy urged me to be there. It brought back some nice memories. I thought about telling her about how I have been speaking to Tommy in church and how he wanted me to visit her and how I felt his Dad took him for a picnic in heaven, but I felt it might create an uncomfortable situation.

Her parents came downstairs for a while. We all just spoke about school and the families. Mrs. Stages told me to tell my family that she would like us all over for dinner one of these nights. I thought that sounded like fun. I told her I would gladly relay the message.

As I was about to leave Mike pulled up into the driveway. I waved hello to him and he offered me a ride. I got into the car and we spoke about the dreams. I told him that the dreams were slow at the moment but I will let him know as soon as I have another good one. I also told him I have the pad, pen and flashlight all ready. He told me to make sure I use them.

When we pulled up in front of the house Mike asked me if my Dad was home. "He should be, c'mon in and see." I told him. We went into the house. Dad just finished talking with Mom about Eddie and the job. Dad and Eddie talked things over on the phone a couple of minutes earlier. Mom couldn't believe the whole situation. She was happy that Eddie was taking it so well.

Mom and Mike talked for a few minutes and then Dad opened up a couple of beers and told Mike to join him in the den. Mike went in and Dad filled him in on the whole Eddie story. The guys hung out in the den and watched the hockey game. Jimmy and me joined them a little later and watched the third period.

At about ten PM. Vinny was finished with his shift. He parked his car in front of his building and stepped out of the car. He yawned and stretched his arms out and turned around. He looked up toward his bedroom window. He became extremely frightened. He stared at the window for close to fifteen minuets. He was looking at a dark figure in his bedroom. It was an outline of a person and it was moving slightly from side to side. Vinny was very nervous. He didn't know if someone was in there or if it was that super natural stuff that has been occurring up there. He decided to head up to the room. When he got to his apartment door he drew his gun. He kicked the door open and searched the entire apartment. Nobody was there. There were broken dishes on the kitchen floor.

Vinny decided that he didn't want to sleep there tonight. He grabbed some of his things and headed back to his car. Before he entered the car, he took another glance at the window. As soon as he looked, he noticed his bedroom light blink on and off and the figure appeared again. Vinny had chills go through his whole body. His hands shook as he tried to get his key in the car door. He finally started his car and he flew over to O'Kelly's. Vinny had a couple of drinks and talked to Brian, the bartender. He didn't mention his apartment to Brian. He decided to call Mike. He knew he could talk to Mike about this type of thing easier than any of the other guys. He borrowed Brian's telephone and started telling Mike what had happened to him. Mike told him that he could spend the night at his place. Once Vinny finished his drink he said goodnight to Brian and went to Mikes.

Mike had the couch all made up for Vinny. The guys had a couple of beers and Vinny filled Mike in on all of the details of his sighting. Mike was amazed. Vinny told him that he was at the end of his rope and that he had to move out of that place. Vinny was in really bad shape and Mike could see it.

The next morning Vinny woke up early. He put some coffee on and went down onto the driveway for a smoke. He was thinking about all of the things that have been bothering him, especially Ted and how he felt like Ted was taking him away from his own case. After he put his cigarette out he went back into Mike's.

Mike was awake, pouring a cup of coffee. "Hey thanks, its nice to have a butler," Mike said as he raised his cup. "No problem, I think I'll have a cup." Vinny replied. "Haunted house shit got you down?" Mike asked. "It's not so much that right now. I was just thinking about how I am being left out of my own case. I am really fed up with that whole thing!" Vinny stated. Mike attempted once again to tell Vinny how that wasn't happening, but Vinny wouldn't listen to it. Vinny went on saying that he would deal with Ted later at O'Kelly's. Vinny left very angry.

At about that time I was visiting the church, I was telling Tommy that I visited his Mother like he wanted me to. I felt his very strong appreciation. I also let him know that his Mother was doing okay. I figured he already knew that but I told him anyway. We talked for a while. Before I left I told him that I was going to walk through the park on my way home from church. I felt a coldness come over me and a strong feeling from Tommy not to walk through the park. The coldness didn't leave until I promised not to walk through the park. I told him I would go straight home and then I said goodbye.

I walked in my front door. "Hello young man, where have you been?" Dad asked. "I was out by church for a while." I replied. "If you want to see Eddie, he will be coming by later." Dad informed me. "What time? I want to make sure I'm here to see him." I asked. "Probably around noon." Dad replied. "I'll be here. Where's Mom?" I asked. "She got an early start, her and Karen went out for breakfast. They'll be back around noon also." Dad replied.

While Mom and Mrs. Stages were out at breakfast they discussed the crisis counseling and some of the other things that have been going on. As they were talking they could overhear a man coughing and choking. It kept getting louder. Everyone in the diner's attention was on the disruption. After a minute or two the choking man came walking past their table on his way outside to get some air.

The man was heavyset. He had an unlit cigar dangling between his thick mustache and beard. Mrs. Stages looked at the man and looked at Mom. "I can't believe it. That guy is everywhere I go." Mrs. Stages said, as she laughed. "I hope he's okay." Mom said, with concern. "He'll be fine, I will probably see him again tomorrow." Mrs. Stages joked. They both laughed.

"Eddie will be over the house later if you want to say hi." Mom informed Mrs. Stages. "Yea, I guess I'll stop over." Mrs. Stages replied. "Who are you kidding? Are you sure I can't take you to the beauty parlor before we go? It's not a secret that you're attracted to him." Mom said. "Does the whole diner need to know? I still feel guilty about seeing anyone. You know what I mean." Mrs. Stages said. "I know, but Jerry understands. It's not like cheating or anything like that." Mom said comforting. "I know, I know.

Let's see what happens when we get there." Mrs. Stages said.

Mom and Mrs. Stages pulled up in front of the house as Dad and me were trimming up the lawn. Mom said hello and went into the house to make us some lunch. Mrs. Stages told us what a nice job we were doing and she followed Mom.

A few minutes later Mom came out to talk to Dad. She asked him if he wanted to invite Eddie and Mrs. Stages to dinner with them. Dad said he would love to. Mom went back into the house with a big smile. Dad and me finished cleaning up and then Eddie pulled up.

Eddie has a beautiful nineteen fifty-seven Chevy, you could tell he just cleaned it. He turned his radio off. He loved to play his Rock and Roll very loud. He got out of his car and came over to give me a big hug. "Hello stranger. It's been a real long time. How have you been?" Eddie asked. "Pretty good. I missed you Eddie. What's knew?" I asked him. "Changing careers, keeping up to date on the Red Wings. Oh that reminds me, I picked you up a puck. It's in the back seat, go get it. There's also something back there for your Brother." Eddie said. Dad walked up to Eddie and warned him that Mom was playing matchmaker and asked Eddie if he wanted to go to dinner with them. Eddie accepted. "The first bottle of cheap red wine is on me." Eddie said, then they went in to talk to the girls.

They made plans for dinner and set up reservations. They decided that Jimmy and me would spend the night at Mrs. Stages's with her parents.

After lunch Jimmy and me watched the baseball game with Dad and Eddie. Mom and Mrs. Stages drove over to Mrs. Stages's house to get all dolled up for their big date. They were acting like schoolgirls; it was good to see them so happy.

At about five PM, after the game, Dad and Eddie drove Jimmy and me over to the Stages's. They dropped us off and picked up their dates. We all said goodnight to each other and they headed out. Captain came in and ran over to us. He was extremely excited. After Jimmy sat down inside, Captain stayed with me by the front door. He jumped up and down and barked. I never seen him this happy. He was jumping up to put his paws on my chest. He howled, and ran around in circles for a while. My only thought was that Tommy was here too. Normally Captain would've walked away sad by now. It was unbelievable. It was just so great to see that little dog so happy after all of this time.

When Captain finally calmed down a little, Jimmy and me hung around with Mrs. Stages's parents. They were also amazed by Captains excitement. We watched TV and played some monopoly. That's my favorite board game. Tommy's grandparents would play monopoly with us every time they came to visit. I was glad we were playing, but there was something missing and even though I felt Tommy's presence, it just wasn't the same.

Dad, Mom, Eddie and Mrs. Stages were having a wonderful time at dinner. Eddie and Mrs. Stages were hitting it off really good. They got to know all about each other and they had a couple of dances together.

At around the same time, Vinny was walking into O'Kelly's to see Ted and the guys. He ran into Bob. They said hello to each other and Vinny asked him if he knew where Ted was. "He's in the back, he should be back in a minute." Bob informed him. "I have to go have a word with him. Is he alone?" Vinny asked. "Yea, he just went to the ladies room." Bob said.

Vinny walked into the bathroom. Ted was washing his hands. "What's going on? What's the story with my case? Vinny asked. "That's my hello?" Ted replied. "With all of the bullshit going on right now, I don't have time for hello's." Vinny said. "Don't explode on me hot shot. I don't need to deal with that type of shit." Ted replied as he turned his back on Vinny and walked out of the bathroom.

Vinny was enraged. He punched the stall door and cracked a piece of it. He walked after Ted "I'm not finished talking with you! You son of a bitch! You don't walk away when." Vinny was cut off as Ted grabbed him by his collar and dragged him to the door. "That's not the way you talk to me, you stupid bastard!" Ted said as he threw Vinny into the street.

Ted went back and sat down. Bob and him continued talking. "What the hell is up his ass?" Bob asked. "You don't want to know. He thinks someone is stealing a case from him, and I also caught him down by the tavern where the evidence is. He was questioning the officers on duty. That's not how you handle." Ted was interrupted by a cold cock to his face. Vinny knocked him down with a cheap shot to the left eye. It caught Ted off guard and he lost his balance and went down off of his barstool. Before anyone could do anything Vinny was out of there.

Bob wanted to grab Vinny, but he had to attend to Ted. Ted got off the floor a little dizzy. "When I get that stupid son of a bitch he is gonna wish he was the kid on trial." Ted said angrily. "Do you want to go looking for him?" Bob asked. "If I don't get him tomorrow, I'll see him Monday, no rush. He ain't going anywhere." Ted replied as he went to clean himself up.

At around the same time, my parents, Eddie and Mrs. Stages were finishing up their drinks at the bar. Eddie and Mrs. Stages hit it off really well and they made plans for next weekend. Eddie dropped her off at around four AM. About an hour after that, I woke up from one of my most memorable dreams ever. It was a good thing I brought my pad with me. When I got out of bed a few hours later this is what I had written.

It's five o'clock in the morning,
Before I say anything else, it is important to know that Josh Owens can make his name look like Eddie Swanson's. He also forgot about his password.
I saw Mr. Stages and Tommy and a heavyset man with an unlit cigar dangling between his thick mustache and beard. Mr. Stages told me that the man was on earth recently, and while he was he helped to keep the wrong men away from Mrs. Stages. If she thinks back to all of the times she seen this man, she will realize each time, he created a distraction. These distractions were made because, at those moments she could've been lured away by men that Mr. Stages did not see as a fit for

her... Is that enough jealousy??? Mr. Stages stressed the fact that he was jealous of all the guys that were about to approach his wife. Since Mrs. Stages is feeling comfortable with Eddie, the heavyset man was finished with his assignment. He passed away a block away from the diner, during his choking fit, which was another distraction.

Eddie has Mr. Stages's approval.

Mr. Stages also gave me some information about a woman who I never seen before. He left a lasting impression in my mind of what she looked like. I felt that I didn't need to write that part down.

Chapter VII

After reading about my dream, the first thing I could think of was to show Mike what I wrote. I knew I would also have to tell Mrs. Stages somehow. I figured I would let Mike handle that. I guess all of these things coming to me had to do with staying over Tommy's house for the night. After all, Captain made me believe that Tommy was there and there wasn't any eriness in my dream this time, except for the heavy guy dying.

How convenient it was that Mike was staying over the garage. I ran up to see him and I woke him up. Although he was tired he was very interested in what I had to show him. He read my paper and he was shocked. He said that we should tell Mrs. Stages as soon as she wakes up. He also said that we should see my Father about Josh and Eddie.

A little while later Dad and Mom pulled up to pick Jimmy and me up. "Oh good, we could get everyone together for this." Mike said. We all gathered around in Mrs. Stages living room and Mike explained why I bring a pad and pen to bed with me. After that Mike read what I had wrote. When he was finished the whole room was silent. The only sound was Mrs. Stages crying.

"That's unbelievable. I can't get over this. Now I could also get to work on Eddie's case" Dad thought to himself.

At that moment the phone rang. Mrs. Stages answered it. "Oh hi Ted. How are you? Good, good. Yea, he's right here, hold on. Bye." She said and gave the phone to Mike. Ted explained everything that happened last night with Vinny. He also told Mike that Vinny went to the precinct early this morning and dropped off his badge and gun and made a scene. He was fed up; he left the force and headed out to live a new life. They didn't even know where to begin looking for him.

Mike told Ted he would be there if he needed anything. "We will probably take a look for him tomorrow, but I really don't care if I ever see him again. I'll give you a call during the week and I'll let you know what's going on." Ted said. They said goodbye and hung up.

"Oh my God! Did anyone hear about a shooting in the park yesterday morning?" Mom asked while glancing through the newspaper. Everyone was interested in hearing the story. "At about nine AM Saturday morning there was a gunman in the park who open fired injuring four people." The paper stated.

I was thankful to be alive. This had to be the reason that Tommy didn't want me to walk through the park. That gave me chills through my whole body. Pretty strange feeling that is. I was also thankful that it wasn't later in the day. Later on that park would've been filled with people.

"Maybe it was Vinny." Mike joked. Then Mike told everyone the story that Ted just told him. We were all surprised by it. We knew Vinny was hot headed and short tempered, but we didn't expect anything like this. Everyone was wondering what Vinny was going to do with his life and where he would go. My Dad thinks he'll be back. He doesn't think Vinny could throw away all that he has here.

Mike then excused himself; he went to call his wife Sarah. Dad said it was time for us to get going also. He was anxious to talk to Eddie. Mrs. Stages asked Dad not to tell Eddie all of the details about the dream. She didn't want to scare Eddie away. Dad told her not to worry.

As soon as we walked in the front door at home Dad got on the phone with Eddie. He told him that Josh was behind the whole mess at work. Dad said that he would try to get some evidence together from work tomorrow so that Eddie could give it to his lawyer.

Eddie was thrilled. He couldn't wait to nail Josh. Eddie was pretty upset that Josh would do something like this to him, he thought they were friends. "I'm glad you believed in me Phil. (Phil is my Dad's name). You could've taken the other side like the other guys, but you're a true friend. Thank you." Eddie told Dad. "Don't worry about anything, the whole thing maybe easier than I thought." Dad replied. They hung up.

At the same time Mike was on the phone with ·Sarah. She was finishing up telling him that she would be on flight two sixty two tomorrow landing in Detroit at two PM at gate sixteen. He told her he would meet her there. "I love you." They each told one another and they hung up.

Mike was happy that he was going to see his wife soon. It has been quite a while since they were together. Mike was just worried that she had to fly by herself. He didn't like to fly, so it bothered him that she had to.

A couple of minutes later the phone rang. It was Bob. He was getting off his shift in a couple of hours and he wanted to see if Mike wanted to get together. "Sure, want to meet at O'Kelly's at around six? Mike asked. "Make it seven. I guess you heard all about Vinny. Isn't that a shame? Bob asked. "Yea, I still can't believe that. He has been pretty strange lately." Mike said. "Let's just see how it all turns out. I'll see you in a little while." Bob said. "Okay, take it easy." Mike replied and they hung up.

When seven o'clock came Mike was at the bar already and Ted walked in. "I didn't know if you were gonna make it. Bob just said he was going to mention it to you. Glad to see you." Ted said, as he gave Mike a hug. "Nice to see you too. What's going on? Is Billy boy coming?" Mike asked. "He might stop by. I don't know if he's working tonight, but if he's not, you know he won't turn down a drink." Ted replied.

"Are you bums gonna order a round, or are ya gonna sit and talk nonsense?" Brian the bartender joked as he set up two beers. "Thanks you bloody Mick." Mike said. "Where were you the other night? Your buddy here got laid out on his ass." Brian said. "I heard. It's a damn shame I missed that. Did he really cry all night, like I heard?" Mike asked.

"Get me a beer, you half a sissy, beer belly bar keep!" Bill yelled out as he walked in the door. "Here you go ugly. Do you want a napkin, so not to get any on your dress?" Brian asked. "Thanks Leprechaun. Did you ladies hear anything good? I heard all of Vinny's mail and shit is being forwarded to his uncle's place in Windsor." Bill said. "We have no reason to even look for that ass anymore. The only reason I wanted to find

66

him was so I could give him a return crack in the mouth. He beat himself up good enough. He doesn't need anymore from me. I'm going to drop it, unless he shows his dirty mug around here." Ted said. "You won't have to worry about that. From what I hear he ain't gonna come back here ever again. That guy has some emotional issues to deal with." Bill said.

"One beer please!" Bob yelled as he walked in. "Welcome old graceful wonder, here's your protector Ted." Brian exclaimed. "I've been going over photos and tire prints for what feels like a week and a half crammed into a day. When we get this son of a bitch my arms are going to be tired from cracking his head open with a baseball bat." Bob said. "Your arms should already be tired enough, lonely boy." Billy joked. "Not as tired as your warped mind after putting together such a clever joke." Bob replied. "Were you able to get anywhere with all of your extra hours today? Ted asked. "I got two new leads." Bob replied, as he handed out two folders. "Mike, you could take one and Billy, you could take the other. I have copies and Ted has enough to keep himself busy. These guys haven't been seen for at least a year. Two separate crimes, one breaking and entering, and the other murder accomplice. They could be promising." Bob said.

"These will bring our total to forty seven checks. I hope these ones bring us closer." Mike said. The guys would get leads every week or so, and as they are on patrol they investigate their new assignments. It isn't part of their current duty; it's to find the killers they are after.

"What's the word on the kid that jumped bail?" Billy asked. "I'm still waiting for the guys on that case to get back to me. They told me the other day that they haven't heard anything new, but once they do they're going to give me a call. That whole thing makes me wonder. If I don't hear anything by Wednesday, I will apply some pressure." Ted said.

Right at that moment a brick came crashing through the front window. Brian jumped over the bar and ran outside. All of the guys followed. Billy pulled out his gun and raised it up over his head. They saw a car in the distance speeding away. Ted ran to his car and radioed to try to get a squad car in the area. Billy and Bob jumped into Billy's car and headed in the direction of the car.

Brian was steamed. He threw his bottle down and it shattered as he cursed his head off. He grabbed a broom and started cleaning up the mess. Mike helped him. "Get a bill together. We are gonna catch this prick and he's paying for your window." Ted said to Brian. "Do you think this is Vinny?" Mike asked. "That's the first one I thought of, but he's gotta be miles away from here by now. He's stupid, but not that stupid." Ted replied.

A couple of hours later Billy and Bob returned. "No luck. We looked all over." Bob said. "I figured that." Mike replied, as he was taping cardboard where the window used to be. "I have a shift in the morning, but I think someone should stay here and watch this place tonight." Ted suggested. The guys looked at each other. "I'll stay, for free drinks. I'm off the next two days." Billy said. "That's a good laddy. I'll be here to pour'em all night, and I'm sure Mr. Glacey will keep us company. Right Mr. Glacey?" Brian asked. "You mmean yourr nnot gonna kick mmee yout tonight? You betta I'll sstay. And I'll beat the ssshit outta whoevadafuk is throwing bricks around." Mr. Glacey replied.

At about nine AM Monday morning Mr. Glacey was passed out with his head on the bar. Billy was still drinking a beer and Brian could hardly keep his eyes open. The Glass Company had just arrived and they were replacing the window.

At the same time Dad was arranging to have one of the other office managers to keep Josh busy so he could go through his desk for evidence. Dad was looking through the last drawer when he came to a folder. He opened it and noticed a few peculiar things. He closed it and put it under his arm and brought it to his office.

He found copies of the check that they blamed Eddie for having issued in his name. There were also papers with Eddie's signature forged over and over. They looked like practice. "How stupid to leave this folder on top of the garbage pail. That's where I found it." Dad just thought to himself, in case anyone questioned how he came across it. Dad called Helmet and told him all about what he came across. He also suggested that they check what password was used on Eddie's computer that day. Just as Dad thought, it turned out to be Josh's password. Dad got that information from my dream.

Dad and Helmet agreed that Josh had to be fired. They also insisted that Eddie should press charges. Dad knew that Eddie wouldn't have a problem with that. Dad and Helmet brought it to Tightass's attention.

Tightass was extremely nervous about the whole thing. He told the guys that he would talk to Josh. Dad was cautious; he wanted to make sure that Eddie and his lawyer were notified immediately so they could press charges. Dad thought that Tightass was covering for Josh.

A little while later Eddie, his lawyer, and a couple of police officers arrived. Josh was placed under arrest. Josh led them to Tightass's office. The office was in shambles and Tightass was long gone.

"That no good piece of shit!" Josh yelled out. Tightass took off with the money that they were able to get away with. That didn't include the five hundred thousand dollars that they tried to nail Eddie with embezzling though. They didn't get that money. They brought Josh in and put out a hunt on Tightass. Josh didn't think that using his own password was a big deal since he had Tightass on his side.

A few hours later Mike was getting nervous because Sarah was in flight and the weather had gotten pretty bad. There was a thunder and lightning storm. He tried to call her when he heard the weather report but she had already left. Mike was a nervous wreck. He called my school and asked if I could meet him for lunch and go to the church with him to say a prayer.

Sarah was in mid flight as the plane went into the storm. She could see the lightning flashing near the windows as the rain was pounding on the wings. The turbulence felt like two gorillas wrestling on top of the plane. Sarah's heart was in her throat and her stomach was flipping and flopping. Passengers began screaming and praying. The engines sounded like they were being turned on and shut off. The lights were also flickering.

A woman across the aisle vomited and that started a couple of others to vomit also. The plane then dropped a hundred feet or so. Sarah grabbed the seat in front of hers and cried and held on for dear life. Everyone was screaming at the top of their lungs. It felt as if the pilots lost control of the plane.

At the same time, Mike was kneeling next to me at the church. I was feeling a long painful and cold distraction for quite a while. I didn't let Mike know about that. I squeezed the seat in front of me and the feeling suddenly turned to happiness and warmth. I let out a sigh and I told Mike that I think everything will be okay.

After what seemed to be an eternity for Sarah, the plane started to straighten out and get back on course as all of the passengers let out a loud relieving sigh.

Mike offered to drive me back to school, but I told him no thanks. I wanted to spend some more time at the church. "Okay, but at least call the school and let them know where you are. I'm trusting you." Mike told me as he ran to his car and rushed to meet Sarah.

After Mike was gone, I had a word with Tommy. I thanked him for the warning about the park the other day. I also asked why I had that strong feeling of pain when Mike and me were praying for Sarah. I felt him tell me that Mike would let me know.

Father O'Reilly came out to say hello to me. I was very happy to see him. I told him all about my latest dream and about the feeling I just had. He told me that it seems like my premonitions are becoming a big part of my everyday life. He seemed very concerned and told me to be careful with that. He asked me how the family and everyone are. I gave him all of the details on everybody and then he let me use his telephone to call school to let them know I wasn't coming back this afternoon. They were okay with it, they understand that I have been busy outside of school lately. I know it doesn't sound normal for school personnel to have that much trust in a student, but they were aware that I wasn't the type to abuse that trust. They also knew what a hard time I was going through these last few weeks.

I was about to walk out of the church and I had a strong heated feeling. I had a vision of myself giving a tour of an old damaged room. The picture was clear, but I don't know what it means. The image stayed in my mind for a while afterwards.

At about the same time, Mike was arriving at gate sixteen as Sarah walked out of the terminal. Mike was never so happy in all of his life. He jumped out of the car and raced to her. Sarah seen him and dropped everything she was holding. She was so excited to see her husband, just a little while before she thought she would never see him again. Mike reached to where Sarah was standing and they embraced with a hug that couldn't fit a shoehorn between them. Tears ran down their faces as they got into the car. Once they started driving Sarah told Mike the whole story of her horrific flight. Mike was beside himself with sympathy for her. Since he doesn't like flying he could appreciate how painful her experience had been. Mike pulled up in front of their temporary home and then gave Sarah the tour.

Chapter VIII

A couple of days passed, it was Wednesday afternoon. Ted was at the precinct. He remembered what he had said about waiting till Wednesday to apply pressure towards the officers on the case of the Camaro driver. Ted got on the phone, "Hey, how's it going? Any good news?" Ted asked. "Hey Ted. I wish I had news for you, but it's not looking good at all. We can't find that guy anywhere. We ran out of places to look. What do you suggest?" The officer on the phone asked. "Oh Jeez. I don't know what to do now. How the hell could he disappear? This doesn't make any sense." Ted angrily stated.

"We questioned the other two that he was with the night he was picked up. They don't know anything. We also questioned his family and searched their houses. They were all upset about the whole situation and it seems like they don't know where he is either but who really knows? They could be covering for him." The officer said.

"Just see if you could find anything, I don't know what else to do right now. I will do what I can on my end. I'll give you a call when I figure something out." Ted said. They said goodbye to each other and hung up.

"Hey Ted, what's going on?" Billy asked as he walked in. "I don't know what the hell is going on anymore. First that asshole Vinny flips out and leaves. Now that driver disappears. How the hell do people just vanish around here? I want to put a manhunt out on this guy. What do you think?" Ted asked. "Run it by the sarge, maybe he'll do it." Billy replied. "I will. I'll leave him a note, he's out someplace now." Ted left a note explaining everything to the sergeant, and asked about a manhunt. Then Billy and Ted headed out. Ted mentioned Vinny a couple more times. It seemed that Ted was really beginning to miss Vinny. He tried to cover it up by talking down about Vinny, but that just seemed like his way to cover up his real feelings. Ted and Vinny were pretty close even though they argued a lot but Vinny was the only one who ever really got away with talking back to Ted.

A little while later Mike and Sarah were at the hospital visiting Stacey Riches, she is the girl that Mike was going to be protecting, but the train hit her bus. They met Stacey's parents. Her Father looks like a military type guy, not too tall but clean cut and strict looking. Her Mother looked older and seemed very sensitive and caring.

Mike and Sarah told them how sorry they are about what happened. They also told her parents how Mike was going to be her bodyguard while she was in town, and that's what brought them to the hospital.

"She looks so helpless. Isn't there anything the doctor could do? I can't take seeing her like this." Stacey's Mother said while wiping her tears. "All we could do is wait. The doctor said to just give positive thoughts and prayers. A coma could last weeks or years. We just have to stay positive." Stacey's Dad said. "She is a beautiful girl. How old is she?" Sarah asked. "Thank you, she's twenty two, she'll be twenty three in September." Stacey's Mother replied.

"I was just about to get some coffee, could I get anything for anyone?" Stacey's Father asked. "I'll take a walk with you, I'd like some coffee. I'll get you a cup too Sarah." Mike replied. Mike and Stacey's Father headed down to the cafeteria and they introduced one another. Stacey's Father's name is Ken. "My wife, Diane can't take this anymore. She is ready to crack. I don't know what to do. I just wish Stacey would wake up." Ken said. "I know it's got to be tough, but you have to stay strong. She could make it out of this. I lost my Godson recently and I can't tell you how tough that was. He was only eleven years old. It was only a year and a half after he lost his Dad. That's what brought me back to Michigan. I'm helping the officers on the case. It was a hit and run driver." Mike explained.

"Wow, that's some pretty heavy stuff. I'm sorry to hear about your loss. I guess you have your hands full also." Ken said. They got their coffees and headed back up to Stacey's room.

Mike and Ken exchanged phone numbers and said goodbye. Mike and Sarah walked to the car and talked about what a nice couple the Riches's are. Sarah mentioned how tough Diane is taking the whole thing. "I am really going to pray for Stacey. I hope she can pull out of this. I can't imagine the thoughts that must be going through the minds of her poor parents right now." Sarah said.

Mike called me later that evening and he told me all about what happened. First he explained the plane ride that Sarah went through. That was what Tommy meant when he told me that Mike would explain the painful feeling I had at the church.

75

I told Mike how I had those feelings and I told him that I was afraid to mention it to him at the church. I didn't want to scare him. When the feeling finally went away, I had that positive feeling that everything would be okay.

Mike also told me to pray as hard as I could for Stacey. He told me that she was the girl in the wreckage from my dream. I told him I would do all that I could. I hope my praying will help.

A couple of days later, the weekend was here. Dad and Eddie were sitting in the den watching the baseball game and discussing what happened at the job. "I can't thank you enough Phil, you really came through for me." Eddie was telling Dad. It turned out that Eddie was able to settle out of court and the company awarded him the amount he was accused of embezzling plus fifty percent. That is a total of seven hundred and fifty thousand dollars. They also offered him his job back, but he laughed at that. There wasn't any way he was going to take that job back, even without Tightass there. Tightass is still missing. Everyone in the office thinks he is lounging on some island in the Caribbean with a girl in one hand and a margarita in the other.

Eddie is going to continue working part time at his Brother's warehouse. With his settlement he will be able to pay off his house, make some investments and live with a clear head.

"You got it my man. I am just happy for you. I told you it could be the best thing to ever happen to you." Dad said. Dad is truly happy for Eddie and Eddie appreciates all that Dad has done for him.

Eddie bought tickets to the Redwings game for all of us for next week, and he said that's just the beginning, we'll be going to a lot more games next season. "What are your plans for tonight?" Eddie asked Dad. "We'll probably get some dinner, nothing too exciting. What about you? What are you and the lovely Karen up to? Dad asked. "We're going roller skating and to a bop dance contest." Eddie joked. He was quoting the Honeymooners. That's Eddie and Dad's favorite TV show.

"Seriously, I'm taking her out for a nice big dinner at The Hong Kong Gardens, no, no, kidding again, uhmmm Filipe's in the city. They are supposed to have the best steak and seafood. I hope she likes it. You know something? I really like her. I hope things work out for us. I still feel a little guilty. I mean I really didn't know her very well when Jerry was here, but I met Jerry a couple of times and I thought he was a really good guy. I hope he understands. I remember the first time I met him. I went to the police station to turn in a gun I found after a crime. It was a very small gun with a red handle. There were initials carved into the handle. I could still remember them, KDL." Eddie went on.

"I'm sure he's okay with you. If he wasn't, some fat guy with a cigar would let you know." Dad joked. "What?" Eddie asked. "Nothing, inside joke, but seriously, I think you guys make a great couple and I hope you stay happy together." Dad said. "I think we will, I may ask her to wear my pin." Eddie said, and they both laughed. That was another reference from The Honeymooners.

"Do you want another beer?" Dad asked. "I would love one but I gotta get going. I gotta make myself pretty, I'm picking up Karen in a little while." Eddie replied. They said goodnight to each other and then Eddie left.

Later on that night Mike and the guys met at Billy's place for a game of cards. Ted was explaining to the guys that the manhunt started yesterday for the Camaro driver. "We're never going to find that guy, not for a year or two, he's got to be long gone by now. That's pretty strange shit how he just disappeared like that." Ted said. "That's one more." Mike said. "One more what?" Bob asked. "One more disappearance. First it was the guy that killed Jerry, then the driver that hit Tommy, and now this guy, who could be the guy that hit Tommy." Mike explained.

"Gimme two cards." Billy said. "What's that smell?" Bob asked. Ted went to the window. "Holy shit, call the fire department!" Ted yelled. "What's going on?" Bill asked. "Your garbage can and tree are on fire!" Ted exclaimed. Billy grabbed the fire extinguisher and ran down with Mike to put the fire out. The flames were getting out of control. Mike unwrapped the garden hose, and the two of them tried to fight the fire.

Neighbors started to come out and they threw dirt and buckets of water onto the fire. The fire department arrived a few minutes later. After they put the fire out they told Billy that this was intentional. They showed Billy a gasoline container that was next to his wall of the building and it would have went up in a couple of minutes if they didn't catch the fire when they did.

Ted immediately called Brian at O'Kelly's. "Keep your eyes open. I think those sons of bitches are at it again. Someone just tried to set Billy's building on fire. It could be the same ones that broke your window. I'll radio the squad car that's sitting by your place. Just be careful." Ted informed Brian. "Thanks a lot. I will keep my eyes open. You take care of yourselves laddy." Brian said. They hung up.

Ted got on the radio, "Okay, okay. I want all of the main roads in and out of town blocked. I want all suspicious drivers questioned. There is an arsonist in the area and we need him caught. Let me know what you find." Ted said over the radio. "I hope someone on patrol nails these bastards." Mike said. "This is strange shit. Someone must have it in for us. We have to check our houses one at a time." Ted said. They checked each house starting with Mike's since his was above Mrs. Stages's garage. They wanted to make sure she was safe too. Everything appeared to be fine over there.

Next they stopped by Bob's place. His house always looked like someone was breaking in. They checked it out and everything was fine. The last stop was Ted's house. Ted went in and told the guys to be careful. The guys headed over to O'Kelly's to check on Brian. Everything there was normal.

Ted went in his house and checked on his wife and kids. Ted has a sixteen-year-old son and a fourteen-year-old daughter. His son's name is Teddy. Teddy is a good kid. He stays out of trouble and does what his Father tells him to do. Ted went into his son's room. His walls are covered with posters of rock and roll bands and girls in bikinis. They talked for a little while. Everything was fine there.

After Ted spoke with his son he went in to see his daughter Rachel. Rachel goes to the same school as me. We're friends; she is just a little strange. She's into the paranormal. Maybe she should spend a day with me. I could show her paranormal. "What happened to Uncle Vinny?" Rachel asked. "What do you mean?" Ted replied. "I have been hearing that he's gone and that he has some problems in his apartment." Rachel said. "Oh boy, you do hear a little more than you need to. Uncle Vinny just had some problems with the job and he is staying with a relative out of town until he works things out. That's all." Ted informed her.

"But I also heard that he was living in a haunted apartment building, is that true?" Rachel asked. "Now that I didn't hear. Where did you hear that?" Ted asked. "I think I overheard Mom on the phone or something. So, is it true? Is his apartment haunted?" Rachel asked. "I don't know what that's all about. There is no such thing as haunted apartments, so don't you worry about that." Ted replied.

Ted talked to Rachel for a little while longer and then he went in with his wife Gail. Ted spoke to Gail about the discussion he had with their daughter. Gail told Ted that Rachel might have overheard her speaking with Mike about the apartment. Ted didn't think that they should be talking about that kind of stuff. Ted considered it nonsense.

A few hours later that night I woke up from my sleep with an odd dream. I wrote it down. It had to do with Rachel and me visiting the church and the church being closed. We tried to get in but all of the doors were boarded up. I attempted to pull a board off of the door, but it wouldn't budge. I turned around and Rachel was gone. I looked around and she was nowhere to be found. I tried analyzing this dream but I couldn't come up with anything. I put the notes in my scrapbook and I figured I would show them to Mike when we get together again.

G. Novitsky

Chapter IX

A couple of days had passed. It's Tuesday and I am in the school cafeteria. I see Rachel sitting with her friends. I decided to take a walk over and talk to her. We said hello and asked each other how things were. "Were you at my Uncle Vinny's apartment?" Rachel asked. "Yea, yea, how'd you know?" I asked. "Oh, I listen to a lot of the phone calls and stuff at my house." She replied.

"Oh, I guess that's a good way to find things out." I said. "So, I hear that some pretty freaky things go on over there at that apartment building. Is that true?" Rachel asked. "You could say that again. I was scared to death over there." I told her. Then I told her some of the strange things that went on over there. She was very interested and she looked like she wanted to hear more and more stories. "Would you be afraid to go back there?" Rachel asked. "I guess not, what do you have in mind?" I asked.

"I like to hear about ghosts and all of that paranormal stuff, you might think I'm strange. Maybe we could visit that apartment and I could see what goes on there." Rachel said. "Sounds okay with me. We just have to keep it quiet and we have to say that we are going somewhere else." I said. "Don't be paranoid, we'll take care of that. Just let me know when is good for you and I'll go with you." She said. I told her that I would get back to her and let her know when would be a good time to go, and then I went back to my lunch.

Later on after school I stopped at Mike's. "Hey, it's been a while, what's new?" Mike asked. "Nothing too exciting, I had another dream. It didn't make much sense." I explained the dream to Mike and I told him that I spoke with Rachel today. Mike mentioned that Ted and Rachel don't see eye to eye on the unexplained. Ted thinks its bologna and Rachel is very interested in it.

"Maybe your dream was telling you that you were going to be meeting with her, that still doesn't explain the stuff with the church though. We'll just have to wait and see if anything comes out of this. Did you make any plans to go to church with her? Maybe you're going to see her there?" Mike asked. "Not exactly. We did make some plans, but it has to stay between her and me." I said. "I'm not sure if I want to hear this." Mike said. "You don't need to, we will be good. Could you tell me, besides what we seen, did you hear anything else about Vinny's apartment? I asked. "Just that it's a place that I wouldn't want to visit ever again. Between that apartment and the kid that jumped bail, Vinny became a complete lunatic. All I could tell you is that Vinny has some freaky stories about that place. There was one night that he said he looked at his window from the street and his bedroom lamp went on. After that, he saw the lamp fall over and it went off. What's your interest in Vinny's?" Mike asked.

"Oh, no reason, Rachel was asking about it." I replied. "Wait a second. Keep Rachel out of the whole thing. She's been asking her parents all about this since I mentioned it to Gail. I never should have brought it up. Now Ted thinks I'm crazy too. Ted's not a believer in things like that. I should bring him to Vinny's and make a believer out of him." Mike said.

"If he doesn't believe by now, he never will." I said. "Not necessarily. He just needs to be shown, I wish he would be shown." Mike said. "Be careful what you wish for." I replied, but it didn't feel like me speaking. It felt like something else inside me made me say that. "I guess your right. I shouldn't wish for something like that. C'mon let me drive you home." Mike said, and we left.

A week later, back at school I was looking for Rachel. I realized that I haven't seen her in a couple of days. I wanted to get together with her. I decided I was ready to take a look at Vinny's apartment with her. After speaking with Mike last week I was pretty excited about seeing the haunted apartment again. I figured we could go by there on Friday after school. I know Mike didn't want me to involve Rachel but I didn't see any harm in it.

After not seeing her all day in school, I decided I should call her from home. "Hello?" Her Mother answered the phone, very upset. "Hi Mrs. Cray, its Stephen McMullen. How are you?" I asked. "Hi Stevie, not so good. It's been two days since we have seen Rachel, Ted has been out looking for her and he can't find her anywhere. Do you have any idea where she could be?" Mrs. Cray asked. I thought for a moment, "Ummm, Did Mr. Cray try Vinny's apartment?" I asked. "No, I don't think so. What makes you think she would be there?" Mrs. Cray asked. "Ummm, Just because she asked about it the last time I spoke to her." I replied. "I will let Ted know to check there if he hasn't already. Can I do anything for you Stevie? Mrs. Cray asked. "No, I was just calling to talk to Rachel. I will keep my eyes out for her. Bye, bye." I said. "Take care Stevie and let your folks know we are looking for her." Mrs. Cray said. "I will." I replied, and we both hung up. I realized that Rachel missing was part of my dream from the other night. Now I am really getting concerned.

I told my parents about what happened with Rachel. They were very alarmed. My Mother let a couple of day's pass before she decided to call Mrs. Cray. She didn't want to make Mrs. Cray have to keep going over the story; it would only make it worse. After those couple of days Mom called to see if she needed anything. "Hi Gail, what's happening? Any good news yet?" Mom asked. "No Julie, I don't know what to do. This is just so horrible." Mrs. Cray replied very upset. "I'm sorry, I just want to let you know, if you need anything at all just give us a call, Phil, the boys, and I are all here for you and Ted." Mom said.

"Thanks Julie, I really appreciate that. It's just so difficult not seeing Rachel come in the door everyday after school and not knowing where she could be." Mrs. Cray started to cry. She thanked Mom over and over again and then they said goodbye to each other. My Mother was very upset after she hung up. She wanted to help but there was nothing she could do except look around for Rachel.

Later on I called Mike to ask him to take me to Vinny's to look for Rachel. "Ted already looked over there. He said the door was boarded up and he had to break it down to get in. That's probably what the boarded doors in your dream were. Ted searched all over for her, but he couldn't find her. He is not taking it well, of course that's expected. Ted has the whole police force out looking for her. Now our search is even bigger." Mike said.

"Yea, you guys have your hands full. Between the hit and run, the gangster, the kid in the Camaro, and now Rachel, It's too much." I said. "Yea, the other things have got to take a back seat for now. Rachel is the most important issue to deal with right now." Mike said. "Yea, that should be the first one you guys find. I hope she is all right." I said. "You better get to sleep I'll talk to you later Stevie. Have a good night." Mike said. "Okay, goodnight." I replied, and we hung up.

I went up to bed, and a couple of hours into my sleep I had another strange dream. I wrote down everything in the dream again.

> Mr. Stages and Tommy are here, they are talking to me, but I can't really hear them. Stacey is with them. She walked over to me. Hello Stephen I am happy to be meeting your friend Tommy and his Father. I would like to stay with them but I am not allowed. I am being sent someplace else. I don't know where it is. I asked Stacey what Tommy and his Dad were saying. Stacey told me that it was very important. She told me to listen to them and call her Father.

After I wrote, I called Mike right away. I told him all about the dream and I told him to call Ken. "Thanks, let me do that. Call me back in twenty minutes." Mike said, and he very quickly called

Stacey's Father. "Ken? Sorry to wake you. Call the hospital, see what is happening with Stacey." Mike told Ken.

Ken called the hospital right away. He had the nurse run in to see Stacey. Stacey's heart had stopped and the nurse rushed to get the doctor on call. The doctors got her heart started with the heart defibrillator. Stacey had been clinically dead for eleven minutes. The nurse told Ken about this. Ken woke his wife up and called Mike back. He told Mike to meet them at the hospital.

Ken and his wife Diane arrived at the hospital before Mike. They ran in to see Stacey. She was coming out of her coma slowly. A few minuets later she began to mumble, "Dad, Mom?" She asked quietly. "Yes, yes dear, we're hear." Diane said. After that Mike entered the room. He said hello to everyone.

"Where's Jerry? Where's Tommy?" Stacey asked. "Who?" Ken replied. "Jerry and Tommy. They were just with me a little while ago. They told me to talk to Stephen. Where's Stephen? Stacey asked. "We don't know honey. Were these guys on your bus?" Diane asked. Mike pulled Ken aside and explained that Tommy is his Godson and Jerry is Tommy's Father and they were the people that he told Ken about the time they met. Ken didn't know how to react. "Stephen is the one that called me. He has been talking to Tommy and his Father in his sleep. He woke up and told me what was happening, that's when I decided that I should call you. Stephen also said that he spoke to Stacey in his sleep. Stephen has special abilities and he and I have been discussing them often." Mike said.

"That's absolutely amazing. I don't know how to thank you and Stephen for saving my daughter's life." Ken said. "Don't worry about that. Just go in and hold your daughter and let her know how much you love her. I will get in touch with you soon. Just do me a big favor, and if she mentions anything at all about Jerry, or Stephen, or Tommy, write it down and hold it until we see each other again." Mike requested. "No problem I will be glad to help you out." Ken said. "Thanks, you guys take care and I will see you soon." Mike said, and then he left.

A little while after Mike returned home, I called him. Once he finished telling me the whole story I became very startled by all of the abilities I started to realize I had. This girl actually died and talked to Tommy and Mr. Stages. She actually spoke to me in my sleep. This is unbelievable. No matter how many times I go over it, it just seems incredibly bizarre. Sometimes you hear stories like this and you figure it's all made up. This time it was all real. I knew that something different has been going on in my dreams, I just haven't been giving it as much thought as I am right now.

Besides all of this, I realized from a dream two months ago that Mike told me he would be gone for two months. This was the dream about the wreckage. This dream was about Stacey. Stacey is the one who was gone for two months. Mike also remembered that part of that dream. "I told you that you had something. I knew these dreams were leading somewhere." Mike said.

I can't even discuss this right now. I am just so amazed by this whole thing. I decided to tell Mike that

I had to get off of the phone. Mike understood. He knew that all of this was too much for a kid to handle.

We hung up our phones. It was about eight AM Saturday morning and I wasn't able to go back to sleep. I figured I would go someplace where I could think about all of this and clear my mind, someplace peaceful and quiet. Yes, the church.

I went inside and I kneeled down by the candles that I enjoyed watching. I closed my eyes to let my mind wander. After about a half-hour I felt like I was able to handle what had happened. I felt like I would be able to talk with Stacey about everything when she comes out of the hospital.

I had one strange feeling though. Normally when I am at the church I have a strong feeling that Tommy is with me. This time I didn't have that feeling. It was just emptiness, not a horrible feeling, just like something was missing.

My mind felt clear enough to walk home. The empty feeling was on my mind as I walked home, but what I really couldn't get out of my mind was the visit from Stacey.

I got home and walked in the front door. Mom was in the kitchen. After she said hello, she went into a rant. "I spoke to Gail today. She's not doing very well. She says that she has been crying everyday since she found out that Rachel is missing. Ted is at the end of his rope also. He is running out of places to look, and the whole force is out of ideas." Mom went on. Mom doesn't know how to help, but she really needs to help. I also wish I could do something. The only suggestion I had was the one that I already mentioned which was that she might have went to check out Vinny's place.

The guys already checked that and they didn't come up with anything.

Ted checked there more than once and he also had Billy and Bob try looking there, and a number of other places. Billy and Bob are not heartless but they feel like their options are running out. Ted has that feeling in the back of his mind also but he could never give up on finding his own daughter.

Ted hasn't been himself lately and he has every reason not to be. He is very angry and irritable. The guys want to help him but the only way to do that is to bring Rachel to him.

G. Novitsky

Chapter X

Later on Saturday afternoon Billy and Bob were discussing the whole Rachel incident with Brian at O'Kelly's. "What can you do? It is a horrible, horrible situation. I am extremely upset about it. I wish I could do more." Brian told the guys. Brian had put up fliers all over and he has all of his customers on the lookout for Rachel.

"If it was a kidnapper we would have had a request for ransom by now." Bob said. "I really have a bad feeling. I hate to even mention it but I can't get the worst possibility out of my head." Billy said. Everything went silent for a moment.

"Gentlemen! What is the word?" Mike asked as he walked in with Dad and Eddie. Dad and Eddie just came in to say hello; they were on their way to the hardware store and a couple of other stops when they ·ran into Mike. "I found these two hoodlums wondering around suspiciously outside. I annoyed the hell out of them until they talked me into letting them buy me a beer." Mike joked.

All of the guys exchanged hellos and handshakes. They were discussing the Rachel disappearance as Brian lined up their beers. Billy motioned to Eddie to let him know he was being admired. In the back of the room there were a few women out having a drink. One of them is a gorgeous red head who is dressed in a way that pleased all of the guys. She had her eyes on Eddie from the minute he walked in. All of the guys began making a fuss over her and they started telling Eddie to get to work on her.

Eddie is flattered but the only woman on his mind right now is Mrs. Stages. Eddie looked to Dad. "You gotta get me outta here. She is gorgeous but she doesn't have anything on Karen." Eddie said to Dad. He said it low enough so the other guys wouldn't hear. Dad nodded as to say he is trying.

"You gotta get some of that. Even if you don't want it, get some for me." Billy said. Eddie tried to laugh it off. He was very uncomfortable telling the guys about him and Mrs. Stages. All of these guys were very close friends with Mr. Stages. Eddie doesn't think they will understand.

"I'll send her a drink from you laddy." Brian said. Before Eddie could stop him, the drink was on its way. After a little while longer of ribbing from the guys and glances from the red head, Eddie had become a nervous wreck. His forehead and palms were sweaty and the worst was just about to happen. The red head came over to thank him for the drink. She approached him with a seductive strut.

Eddie had never been so nervous before. "Hi, I'm Tina. Thanks for the drink." The red head said to Eddie. "Uh, Eddie, um you're welcome." Eddie said as he went to shake her hand. Tina leaned in and kissed his cheek, she was very friendly and easy to talk to. Eddie and Tina spoke for about fifteen minutes before Dad could get him away.

"I gotta get that wood before the lumber yard closes." Dad said to try to free up Eddie. That was a poor choice of words. "If you need wood, Eddie looks like he has plenty." Brian said as all of the guys laughed.

Dad was finally able to get Eddie out of there. Dad knew how difficult this was for Eddie. Tina gave Eddie a kiss and her phone number as Dad and Eddie said goodbye to everyone and rushed out of there.

Tina asked all of the guys about Eddie and his situation. None of the guys except for Mike know about Eddie and Mrs. Stages so they tried to build him up to look even better than he was for Tina. Mike didn't add anything; he just stayed out of it. He didn't know what would be the proper thing to do.

One of Tina's friends ended up hitting it off pretty good with Billy. The two of them talked for quite a while and they discussed getting together for a double date with Eddie and Tina. Of course Eddie didn't have any idea that this date was being planned for him.

On the way to the store Eddie told Dad how uncomfortable he was at the bar. "Thanks Phil, I really appreciate you getting me out of there. Even though it took you long enough, you did it." Eddie said. "Don't mention it. I'm just sorry you can't take a shot at that." Dad said. "I know, it never fails. Something that looks like that will only come around when you know you can't have it. Any other time I would've been waking up next to her in the morning. Damn that sucks, she was hot!" Eddie said. "She's no better than Karen. She just shows everything off. Stick with Karen, she's a better girl." Dad said. "Yea, your right. I know. I was just fantasizing. I just wish Karen knew what I gave up for her. That was a big sacrifice." Eddie said, and they laughed.

"Please don't mention any of this to her. She wouldn't understand." Eddie requested. "What do I look stupid? I've been married for almost sixteen years. If anyone knows that women don't understand, its me." Dad said. They laughed and started discussing their plans for later on.

Eddie told Dad that Mrs. Stages had plans with Sarah and Mom later on, so they decided to get together to watch a game.

While Dad and Eddie were at the lumberyard, I was out with Mom. She had to make a few stops and get her hair done. Usually when she gets her hair done I would go down the block to Lenny's and play the video game machine with Tommy. This time I decided to walk a little further to the cemetery.

I stood in front of the cemetery fence like I do sometimes after school. I glanced towards the graves of Tommy and his Dad. I stared for a while and I suddenly felt Tommy with me. I felt him trying to tell me that the reason I felt alone at the church the other day was because he was giving me time to work out some things on my own. I felt him tell me that if I went to the church right now, he would be there for me. He made me feel a sense of importance in being there. I stood still for a few minutes and then I ran to the beauty parlor. "Mom, I have to go to the church for a little while. I will meet you at home." I told Mom. "Okay, you be careful. Be home soon. I love you." Mom said.

I arrived at the church and I went to my favorite spot by the candles. I kneeled down and cleared my mind. I felt the warmness of Tommy after a few moments. After I shared my happy feelings with him, he started to give me a message. He was telling me that I could find the answer in a certain place. He gave me a mental picture of a place where I should look. He also gave me a route to get there. He wasn't actually speaking; it all came from pictures in my head. Who knows? Maybe I would have had the same thoughts if I wasn't at the church.

It was pretty foggy and quite a long trip. I didn't know what I was supposed to find there. I figured it had to be Rachel. I wanted to head there right away but the next message was that I should go Monday after school with Mike. I'm not going to argue with Tommy. I know that he could see a much bigger picture than I could.

Tommy gave me a sense for what things look like from the other side. It was somewhat blurred but I could feel it was a place that no one on earth could even imagine. He gave me the feeling that all of the things that you would enjoy doing, which you were unable to do here, were everyday activities there.

Later on Eddie came by the house to see Dad. Mom was getting ready to go out with her girlfriends. Eddie and Mom spoke for a little while before she left. Eddie told Mom to make sure she looks out for his girl. "Not a problem. I will give her your love." Mom said and hinted on how great the two of them look together. Mom told Dad she loves him and she said goodbye to all of us.

When Mom arrived at Mrs. Stages's house, Mike, Sarah and Mrs. Stages were all in the kitchen talking about Rachel. They stopped to say hello to Mom. "What's the story with Rachel? Any good news yet?" Mom asked. "No, nothing yet, Ted and Gail are getting worse by the day." Mike said. "That's a shame. Oh Mike before I forget, Stevie said he has something to talk to you about. He said it's really important. He wants to get together with you after school on Monday." Mom said.

"That sounds interesting. I'll give him a call." Mike said. They all talked for a little while and a few minutes before seven o'clock Mom and the girls left for dinner.

Mike called me after they left. I told him all about what happened at the church and we made arrangements to go see the place that Tommy instilled in my head for Monday after school.

After dinner, Mom and the girls stopped by O'Kelly's for a drink before they went home. They sat at the bar and Brian came over. "Top of the evening to you lovely broads." Brian said. The girls laughed. "How have you been Brian? It's been a while." Sarah asked. "Pretty good. Not much has changed since I seen you last. I trust you got my messages from old Mikey boy?" Brian asked. "Oh yes, he gave me all of your hello's." Sarah replied.

Tina walked up to the bar, she was pretty wobbly, she had been there all day. "Let me get another round sweetheart." She said to Brian as she walked by. "Looks like she had enough rounds." Mrs. Stages said. "Be careful how you talk about her, she may be family one day." Brian said. "What do you mean by that?" Mom asked. "Oh, old Eddie boy was in here earlier and she and him hit it off really well. I think they are going to be seeing a lot more of each other." Brian said. "Yea, yea, theya werrr all overrr each slother er todaym." Mr Glacey added. "Oh, is that so?" Mrs.

Stages asked. "Yea, that Tina looked like she was really happy with Eddie." Brian said.

"I have to go." Mrs. Stages said. "Okay, okay. I understand." Mom said. "That son of a bitch is going to hear it from me!" Sarah said. "I'll meet you at the car." Mrs. Stages said. On her way out, she stopped in front of Tina and poured her drink on her. "Dirty slut!" Mrs. Stages said. Mom and Sarah rushed to get Mrs. Stages home. Tina ran and wobbled out of the bar after them but she wasn't quick enough. They were gone.

Mom went home and Mrs. Stages and Sarah stayed up talking at Mrs. Stages's house. Mrs. Stages ended up crying herself to sleep eventually. Her phone rang all night. She didn't answer it. She knew it was Eddie and she never wants to speak to him again.

Sunday morning Eddie was so worried about Mrs. Stages. He called Dad and told him that he hasn't been able to get in touch with her. Mom told Dad that Mrs. Stages was okay, she just has a lot on her mind. Mom was mad at Eddie also but she wasn't ready to discuss what happened with Dad yet. Dad relayed the information to Eddie. Eddie understood but he just wanted to talk to Mrs. Stages so bad.

Eddie wanted to do something to keep his mind off of her, so he went over his brother Kevin's house. Eddie told Kevin all about Mrs. Stages and all of the things that have been going on in his life lately. They decided to spend the day at Hazel Park and catch some horse racing. The guys enjoyed spending some time at the track and watching the races every now and then. They didn't win their bets very often. Kevin liked to play long shot exactas, he figured that was the way to get rich quick.

Monday after school Mike was waiting for me out front. I got in his car and we headed to the store for some snacks for the ride. After we made our stop we headed in the directions that stuck out in my head. We drove for quite a while going by the signs that Tommy had given me. Everything that I was seeing was exactly how Tommy explained it to me at the church.

After about three hours of driving we were a little north of Lansing. That's when I had a sudden feeling of achievement. I started to feel heated throughout my body. I told Mike to slow down a little bit. A little further up on the left-hand side was a small green and white house with a broken down garage near it. I pointed to the house. "That's it! That's the place!" I yelled out. "You sound sure, so I won't even ask." Mike replied. "We have to go in the garage first." I said.

We pulled over a little bit past the house, just in case we weren't welcome. Mike wanted me to wait in the car but I insisted we should go together. Very quietly we headed towards the garage. The doors were locked and the windows had cardboard over them. We couldn't see inside. Mike quietly chipped away at a broken piece of wood and after a few minutes he carved a hole that I could fit through.

I went inside. It was very dark. I looked around to find the door to see if I could open it from inside. There was a car in there taking up most of the space. I finally found the door. It took some strength and twisting and turning but I was finally able to pry it open. I had a very nervous feeling like we were trespassing. I was glad that Mike was a trained bodyguard.

Mike came in through the door. He looked around. He was very quiet while he examined the car. After a few minutes he looked at me. "Do you know what this is?" He asked. "No, what is it?" I asked. "This is the car that hit Tommy." Mike said. He knew that because he spent a lot of time examining Tommy's bike and the tire marks after the accident.

I was in complete shock. What a chilling feeling. "What are we going to do?" I asked. Mike was shaking. "First we are going back to the car. Then we are going to find a phone." Mike said.

We very quietly made our way back to the car. We drove a couple of miles down the road to a small town. Mike found a phone and he called Billy. Mike told Billy that we found the car and he told him to get the guys and get there as soon as possible. He also told him to get the word to my parents so they wouldn't worry.

While we waited we stopped for some dinner and a bathroom. After that we sat down the road from the garage in Mike's car and waited.

After about an hour, two Detroit PD squad cars pulled up. Ted and Bob were in one and Billy and two other officers were in the other. Behind them was a Lansing police car. Everyone got together and they made their plan to enter the house. Bob and Billy went to the door first. They wanted Ted to stay back. He was too emotional; they weren't sure what he was capable of doing.

Billy banged on the door as the other officers surrounded the house. There was no answer. Bob broke the door down and entered. They all had their guns drawn as they searched the house.

Billy came to a door in the basement and he kicked it open. There was a man crouched in the corner listening to a radio. He was surrounded by empty beer cans and liquor bottles. The man looked as if he hasn't showered, shaved or had a haircut in months. His shirt was soaking wet and rolled up in a ball in the other corner. Billy yelled for the others to come down to the basement.

They cuffed the man and brought him outside. I took one look at the man and I lost it. "Oh my God! Oh my God! No! No! It can't be!" I screamed. I was crying my eyes out. The man was Mr. Quinn. Tommy's teacher. I couldn't believe it.

I was silent the entire ride back. Mike dropped me off at home and he told my parents all about what happened. They were in total shock also.

Bob brought Mr. Quinn into the station. Mr. Quinn admitted everything. He was very sorry for what he did. He didn't know what to do after the accident. After going back to school for a few days, the only other thing he could think to do was to run, and that's what he did. In a small way I felt a little bit sorry for Mr. Quinn. It had to be difficult for him. It was an accident. Now he is probably going to spend the rest of his life in jail. That is probably better than the punishment he gave himself in that house over the last few months.

Ted questioned Mike as to what tipped him off to that place outside Lansing. Mike explained to him about my abilities. Ted didn't believe in that kind of stuff, but this made him a little more accepting toward it.

Chapter XI

After a couple more days of missing class, my Mother didn't think it was a good idea for me to continue to be involved in solving crimes with Mike. She wasn't upset with Mike or anything like that, she just didn't think it was a good idea for me to be around those types of situations anymore. Knowing that I had seen Mr. Quinn in the shape he was really bothered Mom. On the other hand, when she thought back to the night in my crib with the walkie-talkies, she couldn't help but think I was somewhat obligated to be involved.

Mike also thought it was too much for me. He believed that Mom was right not to want me involved. He also believes that I am very gifted and I could probably solve all of their cases if I stayed with it, but he also thinks that it is more important health wise for me to live my life like an ordinary child.

My Mother told me that if I could find out where Rachel is, then that would be my last case and then I could retire. I'm glad that she is able to keep her sense of humor after all that went on.

Jimmy came down the stairs. He patted me on the back and congratulated me on a job well done. We got a laugh out of that. "Your lucky, I will never be able to make any changes of activity in the world." Jimmy said. "How would you know?" I asked him. "What do you mean? Its just something you know." Jimmy said. "You could've made hundreds of changes already.

You don't know about them because you only see the outcome that you made happen. You never see what would've happened without your input." I told him. Those were some pretty strong words. I don't even know where they came from.

"Wow. That is some way to look at it. That is deep. I could have made a change every day but I don't know about them because I never seen what would have happened if I didn't change it. That is wild. Where do you come up with this stuff?" Jimmy asked. "It's one of those things my dreams teach me." I told him. "You might not have been born if I did something different than what I did." Jimmy said. "Let's not push it, you didn't create me." I said.

"What if I was a really rotten kid? Do you think Dad and Mom would have had another one?" Jimmy asked. "It could be like that, or maybe they wanted to try to have the opposite of what they already had." I said.

We both laughed. We learned something about each other that day. We also felt a little closer. From then on Jimmy also thought about how things could change just by what time we wake up or by what we decide to eat or drink or when we decide to eat or drink it. Maybe our little talk that day changed the world around us a little more.

After our discussion the phone rang. "Hello? Hey, what's up Eddie? I haven't heard from you in a while." Dad said. Eddie told Dad how depressed he has been over the last few days since he hasn't seen or heard from Mrs. Stages. "I know I'm the last one with an excuse for depression after I was awarded that money and I have bar chicks hitting on me, but I really miss

Karen. Do you think someone mentioned Tina to her?" Eddie asked.

"That's a good question. I'll have to see what I could find out." Dad said. "Thanks, I really owe you for everything. You have been helping me out left and right lately. I don't know how to thank you." Eddie said. "Set me up with Tina." Dad joked.

They talked for a while; Dad let him know all about Mr. Quinn and how they didn't want me to be involved in all of that anymore.

After Dad hung up the phone he went in to see Mom. "What's wrong with Karen?" Dad asked. "Nothing, why?" Mom replied. "Eddie and her were having such a great time together and now all of a sudden she doesn't want to talk to him anymore." Dad said. "Let me tell you something about your pal Eddie. I didn't want to bring this up yet, but now I guess I have to. Your friend Eddie was out with another girl a few nights ago." Mom said. "Where did you hear this? Eddie has been with her or me or us the last few days, when could he have had time for another girl?" Dad asked.

"Brian at O'Kelly's told us about her when we stopped in the other night. He said that Eddie and that girl were all over each other. We even seen the girl, she is a tramp." Mom said. Dad started to laugh. "That's funny, I should have known. So it's all about Tina? Oh boy, the other day Mike brought Eddie and me into the bar. That girl started hitting on Eddie from the second he walked in. Eddie practically lifted me up to get away from her. He made me tell the guys how busy we were so that I could get him out of there. All that he did was talk about how much he loved Karen and how he wanted to get away from that girl so not to mess things up with her. It figures. If he would've done something with her, everything would probably be fine, but he worried and panicked about it, now he gets blamed for cheating on her. I think you should try to straighten it out with Karen. I would like to talk to her too." Dad said.

"What a shame. I had no idea. I will call her. I will try to fix it. Stick around I may need you." Mom said. Mom tried calling a couple of times but there was no answer. She said that she would try again later.

Mrs. Stages didn't answer the phone because she was out. She decided to go out for a walk by the lake where her and Mr. Stages used to go. She sat by the water and talked to Mr. Stages. She told him how much she misses him and she questioned him as to why all of these strange things were going on. She also wanted to know why he gave Eddie approval and then Eddie treated her so terribly. She stayed by the lake for a few hours. She didn't get any answers to her questions, but she got a feeling of tranquility from being there. She decided she was not going to stop going to the lake.

She had stopped for a while because the thought of being there without Mr. Stages made her sad. Now she believes that Mr. Stages is still there and he gives her that tranquil feeling. She decided to forget about Eddie. She was really starting to fall for him but she believes this has been a message not to get involved with anyone else.

The next day, Mom was finally able to get in touch with Mrs. Stages. Mom tried explaining what really happened at the bar. Mrs. Stages didn't want to believe any of it. She explained all of her feelings about it to Mom. Mom was very upset that Mrs. Stages and Eddie were not going to work it out, but if that's how Mrs. Stages felt, Mom was not going to intrude.

Mom felt really bad that it was her idea to try to get the two of them together in the first place. After they spoke about all of that, they made plans to get together for lunch over the weekend.

Mom told Dad all about what she and Mrs. Stages discussed. Dad was pretty annoyed that Mrs. Stages was going to give up over a misunderstanding, but he wasn't going to intrude either. Dad told Mom that he would break it to Eddie when they get together for the game later.

Back over the garage at the Stages's, Mike was on the phone with Mrs. Cray, Ted's wife. She is still very distraught and she informed Mike that there still hasn't been any luck in locating Rachel. "We're still looking, you have to try to keep a positive outlook. I still believe that we are going to get her back to you, and soon." Mike told her. Mrs. Cray thanked him for all of his support and then she started to ask about the situation with me. "I hear that poor Stevie is pretty shaken up and he won't be able to give anymore insight toward solving cases." Mrs. Cray said.

"I really don't think he should be around any of this anymore, it's too much for a kid his age, hell it's too much for people our age. I spoke with his Mom. She says that she doesn't want him involved, unless he has some information that will lead us to Rachel. If he could help find her, Julie will be more than happy to let him be involved." Mike said. "That's good to know. I hate to burden everyone with it. I just want my little girl home safe again." Mrs. Cray replied as she let out some tears.

"That's what we all want and that's what you're going to get." Mike said. "I hope your right. I can't take it anymore, and poor Ted is at the end of his rope. He doesn't sleep, he walks around in a daze and he doesn't talk anymore, he just grunts. I found him yesterday standing in front of Rachel's bedroom door just staring in for the longest while. He has got me nervous too." Mrs. Cray explained.

"That is so upsetting. I guess he's still not able to come to the phone?" Mike asked. "No I'm sorry, I still can't get him out of the basement. He spends most of his time down there when he's not working. The sergeant has been giving him extra time off and I think he is going to give him a leave of absence. He is also going to have the police psychologist meet with him. Please don't mention that to the other guys. They will probably find out sooner or later, but I think later is better." Mrs. Cray said.

"Don't you worry about that. I won't say a word. Besides I think it's a good idea. Maybe that will help him out a little. You should go with him. It usually helps to do those things as a couple." Mike said.

"Thanks a lot Mike, you're a big help. I will let you know what's going on and I'll say hello to Ted for you." Mrs. Cray said. "You take care and I'll do all I can for you." Mike said, and they hung up.

Mrs. Cray turned around and her son Teddy was standing behind her, with his eyes filled with tears as he asked if there was any news about Rachel. He knew the answer was no, but he had to ask anyway. Teddy is also pretty messed up about the whole situation. He is very worried about the way his Father is handling it. He and his Dad have always been very close, now they hardly even talk.

"Just keep praying honey, Mike and the guys are still looking. They are not about to give up and I don't want you to either. Why don't you give Stevie McMullen a call? I think he'll be able to make you feel a little better." Mrs. Cray said. "Okay Mom, I'll call him after dinner. Thanks." Teddy replied. Teddy didn't know how I could make anything better, but he figured anything was worth a shot.

Teddy and me ended up talking for a while after dinner. We didn't know each other that well, but after our conversation we knew a lot more about each other. I didn't give him all of the details about what had been going on with me lately, but I gave him an idea about it. Teddy informed me of all of the details about his family and how much they were torn apart by the loss of his little sister.

Once I was about to get off of the phone, Eddie walked in. He patted me on the back, said hi and stopped by the fridge. Then he went in to see Dad. "Phil, how the hell are ya?" Eddie asked as he shook hands with Dad. "Not bad, it's good to see you smiling." Dad replied. "Crying never helps. Right?" Eddie asked.

They talked for a while and then Dad informed him about how Mrs. Stages decided to handle their situation. Eddie was pretty disappointed, but he figured he couldn't change her mind. Everyone pretty much thinks it's better to back away from making decisions for Mrs. Stages since she has so much on her mind lately.

"I know she has been through a lot and all. I know it may not have looked good but if this is her adult way of handling the situation, maybe I'm better off without her. It might sound like I'm trying to sound tough about it but that's the way I feel right now. Sure I love her, and I wish all of this didn't happen this way. I'll probably be very depressed for a few weeks but I think it is pretty damn immature of her to not even want to hear what I have to say about it." Eddie went on.

"I hate to see something that seemed so good end too, but your right. I am not going to tell you to go crawling back to her if she won't even take your phone calls." Dad said. "Yea, we could talk about her another time, put the game on. I brought some beers; they're in the fridge. I'll go get us a couple." Eddie said as he walked into the kitchen.

Eddie and Mom met each other in the kitchen. They both felt a little awkward. They spoke for a couple of minutes but neither of them mentioned Mrs. Stages.

Later that night, once again I woke up in the middle of my sleep. I had a dream that reminded me of the situation at the church that led us to Mr. Quinn. It started with Teddy Cray asking me for help. I went to bed thinking of him because of our earlier phone call. He came to me and told me that if I don't find Rachel, his Father will put me in jail. We started walking to his Fathers' precinct. On the way there he pointed out some landmarks. It was an incredibly long trip. It seemed like we were walking for days. I woke up remembering where he took me, and how we got there. I wrote down some notes also.

I thought about calling Mike to let him know about it, but I didn't think it was quite enough information for me to get myself involved again, especially if my parents found out. I decided to keep my notes and hope for a part two of this dream, or maybe I could have a word with Tommy at the church and see what he thinks.

I tried desperately to get back to sleep to continue the dream, but I could never dream when I want to. The dreams only come when they're ready to. I did go back to sleep though. I woke up at around ten o'clock Sunday morning. I decided to stop by the church after breakfast.

Mom didn't mind that I visited the church, she just didn't want me getting involved in any police type activity. "Be careful and come right home when you're finished at church." Mom said. I told her not worry as I headed out.

When I arrived at the church, there was a mass underway upstairs. I stayed for a little while to hear the Gospel. It was about teaching others how to see things for what they truly are. How a profit showed the apostles the truth that was hidden behind signs. Anyway, that's how I interpreted it. I felt like it was directed towards me personally.

The priest then said his Homily. He spoke about Pontius Pilate. I heard the name before but I was unsure who he was until now. Pontius Pilate was the local Roman magistrate in charge of Jerusalem. King Herold sent Jesus to Pilate to have the Romans deal with him as an enemy of the state. Pilate then gave the Jewish citizens a choice to free Jesus or to free a murderer and a thief named Barabus. The citizen's chose to free Barabus and to have Jesus hung on the cross. Pontius Pilate said that Jesus has done nothing wrong, his crime was claiming that he was the Son of God. Pilate then asked for a bowl of water to wash his hands of Jesus's death. I don't understand why they made the decision that they did. That is just another way to see that certain decisions can change everything. From what I learned about Pontius Pilate made me believe that he wasn't a bad man.

After the Homily, I went downstairs to where it was quiet. The candles that I liked were upstairs but there were also some candles downstairs. I figured they would have to do. I started talking to Tommy quietly and I closed my eyes. After a little while I had that feeling that Tommy sat next to me. I asked him about my dream but he didn't have anything to add to it. For some reason I started to think about the time his dog Captain was acting wild when I walked into Tommy's house. That was the day I felt that Tommy was with me.

I just started to feel Tommy trying to tell me that he really was there that day. I felt him tell me that he thought his Mother looked beautiful that day. That gave me a chill down my spine. Tommy thanked me for going there and informed me that his Mother was on the verge of a nervous breakdown and my visit prevented it.

On my walk home from the church, a car pulled up next to me and stopped. "Hey Stevie!" a voice came from the back seat. I looked over. It was Teddy Cray. "Hey Teddy, how's it going?" I asked him. "Not too bad. Do you need a ride?" Teddy asked. "Uhm, yea, I guess." I replied, as the door opened for me. One of

Teddy's friends was a little older; he was old enough to drive. Teddy introduced me to his two friends, Richie and Jason. They seemed nice. I started to tell Teddy about my dream as I also told Richie how to get to my house.

Teddy was very interested, especially since he was a main character in the dream. "If you remember how to get to the place in your dream. Richie could drive us. I mean, since you don't want to get any adults involved, we could check it out ourselves." Teddy suggested. "Hey, that sounds like a pretty good idea, but I can't tell my parents that we are going to look for your sister. Or, maybe, wait, that might be the perfect thing to tell them. It wouldn't be a lie and they already know that you guys go out looking for her." I said.

We decided that we had a plan. I brought all of the guys in to meet Dad and Mom. They liked to know the kids that I would be hanging around with. We just explained that we were going to drive around the neighborhoods to all of the places that Rachel may have ended up.

"Be careful, and call us if you're going to be late." Dad said. We told them that everything would be fine and we headed out.

It took a while to find the spot where my dream began, but once we found that spot I felt like I was back in my dream. We drove for about two hours or so before we got to the little town that I dreamt about. Teddy's friends were not very positive about our journey, but they stuck with it. Once we were inside that small town, we found a pay phone and I called to let my Dad know that everything was okay and we were going to stop for something to eat.

"Okay, very good. Thanks for the call. Don't eat any garbage, make sure you have something healthy." Dad said. After Dad hung up he told my Mother that everything was fine and that he thinks it's a good idea for me to get out for a while with other kids, even though they are a little older than me.

We ate at a diner. On our way out of the diner a woman was on her way in. It was the woman that Mr. Stages pointed out to me in my dream. I was stunned for a moment and I stepped back. The woman then noticed me staring at her. "Do I know you young man?" She asked. I paused for a moment. "N, na not really. I was given a message for you though." I said. "Really, what is it?" She asked. "Don't think I am strange or anything but about a year ago you were at work. There was an announcement of a gas leak in your building. They sent everyone in the building home for the day. You were very, very aggravated because you had so much to do." I said, as she had a very surprised look. "You are absolutely right. I still get annoyed when I think of that. How did you know?" She asked.

"That is not all. You went home early that day. Your husband was there when you got home. You used the time to get close to each other. You shouldn't let the gas leak annoy you. If it wasn't for that gas leak your little baby Kenny would not have been delivered nine months afterwards." I said. I wasn't sure about this story while I was telling it to her, but then I seen a tear roll down her face and she hugged me. "I don't know who you are or how you know this, but that is exactly true and I never realized how I was being angry at that gas leak when it was the best thing that ever happened in my life." She said.

That gave me the greatest feeling. It was very touching. The woman just stood there for a while as her friend was waiting for her at the door of the diner. I walked away as she just seemed mesmerized and I got into the car to continue our trip.

As we got a little deeper into the town, everything seemed too easy. The apartment complex was right where it was in my dream. I didn't think we were going to find anything. We found this place too easy, but I did have the same feeling that I had when we found Mr. Quinn, so I was a little nervous.

We parked the car outside of the complex. The complex is pretty warned down and not kept up very well. It looked like a cheap Motel. We walked to the last door on the third floor hallway. That is where all of my feelings brought us. Teddy knocked on the door. There was nothing. He started knocking harder, and there was still nothing. "Should we leave?" Teddy turned around and asked. "I don't know." Richie said. I started to feel a large sense of failure. How could I drag these guys all the way out here for nothing? I started to doubt my gift.

We all stood and looked at each other for a few seconds. The guys made me feel guilty about bringing them here. My right arm started to tremble with fear as I broke a sweat. The guys worried, as my face became pale. My entire body became heated. "Break the damn door down!" I yelled out. The guys looked at me like I was crazy, but they figured that I brought them here, so I must know something.

They all started pounding on the door and kicking it. We started to hear a muffled scream from inside. Richie ran to the car to get his tire iron. We all kept kicking and pounding. Richie got back and he was able to start a hole in the door and he also broke the doorknob off. We finally got inside. We ran to where the sound was coming from. Then we had to break down a closet door, and there we seen Rachel duct taped and tied to an iron safe.

There was a bowl of dog food and a bowl of water next to her. I didn't even want to imagine her eating from that. Teddy broke down into tears, he was so happy to see his Sister. We were able to free her, she grabbed on to Teddy, she didn't say a word, she just held on to him and cried.

"Lets get the hell outta here before whatever animals did this come back and kill us!" Richie exclaimed. Everyone agreed and we got Rachel to the car and flew back towards the highway. Rachel was wet and dirty, she had scrapes and bruises all down her arms. She looked as if she had been through a war. She didn't say a word during the two-hour ride back. All she did was hold onto Teddy like she never wanted to let go. We tried to get the details from her, but we understood that she didn't want to talk about it and she would probably never want to tell anyone about it.

I knew that Teddy was going to be out for revenge, not to mention his Dad. I know his Dad is going to be out for blood. That's what worried me.

Once we were a couple of blocks from Teddy's house, we all had a nervous, excited feeling. Teddy just couldn't wait to get out of the car and make the announcement. Richie and his friend Jason were just stunned from the whole ordeal. I was a nervous wreck. I don't know if my parents are going to be mad or not when they find out that we followed another one of my dreams, or are they just going to be so thrilled that I helped find Rachel?

We pulled up in front of Teddy's house. Mrs. Cray took a look out of the front window and as soon as she realized it was Rachel that she was looking at, she ran out of the house screaming like a fanatic. Mrs. Cray and Rachel ran to each other and embraced. Mrs. Cray was overwhelmed. The two of them held onto each other as if they would never separate ever again.

All of the commotion caused the neighbors to start pouring out of their houses into the street. Everyone was very excited to see Rachel home safe; they didn't want to bother the family reuniting though, so they watched from a distance.

For a moment everything went silent. Every ones attention was focused towards the Cray's front door. We all looked to see Mr. Cray standing there in disbelief. The commotion took him away from the basement where he had been hibernating lately.

Once Mr. Cray realized what was happening, his eyes filled up with tears of joy as he began to make his way to his Daughter. We all parted to let him through. I thought Mrs. Cray held Rachel close. When I saw Mr. Cray hold onto her, I thought she was going to break in half.

At that point all of my fear and nervousness just disappeared. The happiness that I helped create for this family was worth any anger my parents could ever have.

When things started to calm down a bit, the word spread like wild fire. People ran to their phones to tell their family and friends what just happened. Before I knew it, Mike was there. Mike took one look at me and he winked. "I know this had to be your work." Mike whispered to me as he came closer. "Yes, it was part of another dream, I was going to call you but, I didn't feel that it was enough information at the time." I explained to Mike. "Don't be silly, you did it. That's all that matters." Mike replied.

As Mike and me spoke to each other, he brought up how he mentioned a while ago that he hoped Ted would become a believer. I remembered exactly what he was talking about. That was the time that I told Mike to be careful what he wishes for. Now we both understood why I said that.

Teddy just finished explaining the whole story to his Dad. He told him all about my dream and how I have some kind of special ability. Mr. Cray was lost for words. He walked up to me and gave me a big hug. Then he looked to Mike. "Now I'm a believer!" Mr. Cray stated.

Just then my parents pulled up with Jimmy. After everyone gave me hugs and thankful thoughts, my parents just seemed so proud of me that I didn't worry at all about how I thought they were going to feel.

They were just too excited to care how it happened. After all of the excitement, Mr. and Mrs. Cray brought Rachel to the hospital to have her checked out completely.

Chapter XII

The following day my parents told me how proud of me they were. We discussed thoroughly how I helped discover Rachel. It seemed like they forgot all about the fact that they didn't want me involved in solving cases anymore. I didn't bring it up. If they weren't going to mention it, I sure wasn't going to either.

Over at the hospital Rachel was doing a little better. After the doctor looked her over he let Mr. and Mrs. Cray know that everything is going to be okay, physically. He recommended that she see a psychologist or a therapist for her recent emotional difficulties.

Mr. and Mrs. Cray were very thankful that Rachel didn't have any physical ailments, however they made sure to make an appointment with a therapist. They decided to go with a recommendation from the doctor.

For the next few days Mr. Cray attempted to get some information from Rachel about the place she was taken to, but she still wasn't discussing it. Mr. Cray didn't want to pressure her after all she had been through. He was able to get all of the details that he needed from Teddy. Now he could make plans to visit that place.

I didn't want that to happen but I knew it would eventually. In a way it was pretty exciting to me that the guys were going over there looking for some action. On the other hand, it was also pretty frightening.

I wonder what is going through the minds of the animals that did all of this. They are sure to return to that apartment and discover Rachel is not there anymore. When that happens, I'm positive they are going to leave town. Mr. Cray probably won't even have a chance to get even with them.

I figured I should give Mike a call and share my feelings with him. Maybe he also has some information to share with me.

Mike is in his apartment on the phone with his security friend Roy, who is covering for him down in Florida. Mike calls to check on him from time to time. "Everything is pretty good. Nothing to worry about down here. How is it going up there? Any luck yet?" Roy asked. Mike informed Roy about all that was going on up here. Roy was amazed at how much had been going on in such a short while.

Right after they finished up their discussion is when I called Mike. "Hey Mr. crime solver, what's knew?" Mike asked me. I told him that everything is going pretty good and I told him how I felt about the apartment complex.

"You have a good point. We were thinking about taking a ride up there tomorrow. Ted is pulling Teddy out of school for a couple of days. He is supposed to show us how you guys found that place." Mike said.

"I hope Teddy remembers how to get there. It is a pretty confusing trip." I told Mike. "We will find out soon enough." Mike said.

The next day Mr. Cray, Teddy, Mike and Richie took a ride out there. They brought three other police officers in a separate squad car. Teddy and Richie couldn't remember all of the details to find the place so they called me about ten times on their way up for some assistance. Their ride took a lot longer than it took us the first time.

After a long four and a half-hours of driving they finally came to a familiar looking area. "This is it, there's the apartment complex!" Richie exclaimed. "Okay, lets all be cool. I'm going to park a little further away and you and Richie are going to sit in the car." Mr. Cray told Teddy.

They parked a decent distance from the apartments. Mr. Cray and Mike discussed their plans with the other officers. Mr. Cray, Mike and two of the officers made their way up to the apartment. The other officer stayed close to Teddy and Richie by the cars. That officer radioed to local police to have a car come by in case they needed back up.

Mr. Cray busted the door down and they all entered cautiously with guns drawn. The apartment was in shambles. They could tell that whoever was there made a run for it. They searched for whatever evidence they could gather up.

When they were finished collecting evidence and dusting for finger prints Mike and one of the officers headed to the building manager's office. Mike found out that the room had been rented to a man named Muekaz and he has only been there for a few months. It turned out that another apartment in the complex was also rented to Muekaz. Once the guys heard that, they headed to that apartment. The second apartment was in the same condition as the first. They gathered evidence from there as well.

Mr. Cray is very suspicious about the whole situation. He sat down with the building manager. The building manager put on a pot of coffee for the guys. Mr. Cray asked him for any details he could supply on Muekaz. He informed Mr. Cray about Muekaz's daily routine and about the friends he had staying with him. "They were pretty quiet but they were in and out all of the time. There were about five or six of them in and out of both of the apartments. They didn't seem to make any trouble, so I never questioned them. I got my rent money on time so I was happy." The building manager told Mr. Cray. He also informed Mr. Cray that there is a shed in the back that they used to go in and out of. The manager let them use it for supplies and things.

Mr. Cray decided to take Mike and have a look at the shed. There were tools and some gasoline containers lying around in there. When they were leaving the shed they saw the local police going through the apartments with a K-9 unit. They had the dog sniffing around for anything suspicious. "When your done up there, let him give the shed a sniff." Mr. Cray yelled out to the officer.

The three officers that came out with Mr. Cray and Mike were rapping things up and saying goodbye. Mr. Cray and Mike were just doing some paperwork. They sat by the car for a little while and all of a sudden they heard barking. One of the local officers yelled to the guys to come back to have a look.

They all got to work digging. Deep under the shed a body turned up. Not only were they confused about the whole situation, now Mr. Cray was starting to feel sick. He could only think about how this could've been his Daughter's body if we didn't get there in time.

The body was in pretty bad shape, his own parents wouldn't even recognize whoever he was. All they could tell was it was the body of a male. Before everyone left they waited for the coroner and they told him to give this body special attention at the autopsy.

Later on after everything calmed down a little, Mike got a phone call from Ken Riches, Stacey's Dad. "Hello Mike, how have you been?" Mr. Riches asked. "Wow, Ken, hi. So much has been going on. I don't know where to start." Mike replied, then he filled Mr. Riches in on what was happening. Mr. Riches didn't know how to respond. Everything that has been going on is just not normal. "It sounds like you have your hands full, maybe you should have a seat." Mr. Riches said. "What do you mean?" Mike asked.

"Stacey has done some writing like you suggested. It's all Greek to me but maybe it will make some sense to you." Mr. Riches said. "Oh boy, I am anxious to see it but also a bit nervous. Why don't we meet for coffee whenever is good for you?" Mike asked. "Sounds good, I am off tomorrow, how about nineish? Mr. Riches replied. "That sounds perfect." Mike said, then he made sure that the usual coffee shop was okay with Mr. Riches.

The next day Mike arrived at the coffee shop at nine o'clock on the dot. He saw Mr. Riches sitting in a booth in the corner by the window having coffee. "Glad you could make it. How are you?" Mr. Riches asked Mike. "Not bad, nice to see you too." Mike said as he sat down across from Mr. Riches.

Mike ordered a cup of coffee and a sandwich as they began talking. "I'm pretty hungry, aren't you going to eat something?" Mike asked. "I have a bowl of soup on the way." Mr. Riches replied, as he pulled a piece of paper out of his pocket. "I guess this is what your Daughter wrote." Mike said as he opened it. It said:

After they visit the third floor, the dog will find the body that you buried in the shed. You're not going to be able to stop the information obtainer.

Your friends can cast stones or spread flames but that will not even any score. Billy won't let you get away with it.

You can't hide your K D L forever.

"It doesn't make complete sense but some of this stuff is right on the money." Mike said. "After she finished, she handed it to me and told me that she can't write anymore. She doesn't know who the message is for and it is scaring her. She really hopes that she is finished as a messenger." Mr. Riches said.

"I really don't want to see her getting pain out of this. Why don't you just tell her that what she wrote was a big help and I don't think there is any other information that she could possibly be given? Maybe that will get it out of her mind." Mike suggested. "Sounds good. I'll give that a shot." Mr. Riches replied.

Back at the Cray's house Teddy and Rachel were home from school with their parents. Mr. Cray is not scheduled to go back to work until Wednesday. That gives them five days to take a small trip to clear their heads and give them some much-needed time together.

They scheduled Rachel's next trip to the psychologist for next Thursday. The psychologist, Gary, thought it was a great idea for them to have a little family getaway.

Mr. Cray decided that down near Beavercreek would be a good place to get away to. Mr. and Mrs. Cray started to put some plans together. They planned on leaving first thing in the morning, at about six AM.

Rachel has been coming around quicker than expected. She only had one visit with Gary so far and they haven't discussed the day of her kidnapping yet. She has been running around the house and even laughing once in a while. It looks like she is going to come out of this whole thing pretty good.

Later that night Bob and Billy stopped over to see the Cray's. Billy just finished his shift and Bob starts his in about an hour. They came by to make sure everything was okay with Rachel and they dropped off a small gift for her. They also wanted to say goodbye before the Cray's left for their vacation.

"Do you fellas want a little something to eat?" Mrs. Cray asked. "No thanks I had a big lunch." Bob replied. "I don't mind if I do." Billy said as he grabbed a hamburger off of the stove.

"How is she holding up?" Bob asked. "She's doing much better than we expected." Mrs. Cray said. "That's great. I don't think I would have bounced back that quick." Billy said with his mouth stuffed. "Don't talk with your mouth full." Mr. Cray said as he walked into the kitchen.

"There's the old man." Billy said as he shook Mr. Cray's hand and patted him on his back. "It's great to see you back in good spirits. I hope you enjoy your ass off on vacation." Bob said. "We are all going to enjoy our asses off this weekend!" Mrs. Cray said as she handed the guys a can of beer each. "Thanks dear." Billy said. "Thanks, only one for me though, I am on my way to work." Bob said. "Why don't you guys make yourselves comfortable inside?" Mrs. Cray suggested. They headed into the den and Mr. Cray gave his wife a kiss on her forehead.

The guys talked in the den for a while before Bob had to get up and head to the precinct. He said goodbye to everyone and he made sure he gave Rachel a big hug. "Hang in there little soldier." Bob told Rachel.

"So, what are your plans for tonight?" Mr. Cray asked Billy. "You'll never guess, did any of the guys tell you about the girl I hit it off with at O'Kelly's? She is friends with the girl that was all over Eddie." Billy said. "Yea, I remember hearing something about that." Ted replied. "I am taking her out tonight. Her name is Donna, she has an apartment not too far from here." Billy said. "Sounds good, I hope it works out for you two." Ted said.

Teddy came into the den to say hello. "Hey big man, look at you. You get taller every time I see you." Billy said. The guys talked and watched the baseball game before Billy took off for his date.

Billy picked Donna up at her apartment. He walked her to his car and they headed off to the movies. While they were driving, Billy was distracted looking in the rear view mirror while Donna was talking. "What's the matter?" Donna asked. "I seen that car on my way to your apartment and now its behind me again." Billy said. "How do you know it's the same car? Oh yea, you're a cop." Donna said. "Ha ha, funny. I'm not positive, hold on a second." Billy said as he picked up his radio. "Bob, you there? Bob come in." Billy said. "I'm here." Bob replied over the radio. "I need you to run a plate for me when you get back to the precinct." Billy said. "Let me have it." Bob replied. "Its 2CB-8U1 Michigan, oh shit, he's turning off. He might have seen me on the radio." Billy said. "I'll give it a run when I get back to the station. I'll call you at home later." Bob said. "Thanks buddy, I'll talk to you later." Billy said.

"How exciting!" Donna said. "Wise ass." Billy replied. "No, I'm serious. Police talk turns me on." Donna said. "You don't say? Well, I had a seven twenty one and an eight forty six last night." Billy joked. "How'd you like a big sixty nine tonight?" Donna joked back. "Affirmative ma'am." Billy said. They drove around to see if they could find the car that was following them but they didn't see it anywhere.

Later on that night while everyone in my house was sleeping, I woke up in a cold sweat and went downstairs. I headed outside through the back door to get some fresh air. I was looking around the backyard; it was pretty foggy out. I gazed toward the old tin shed all the way in the back by the fence between the bushes. The doors of the shed were open. I noticed an outline of a small person standing between the doors. It caught my attention as I just froze and stared. My normal reaction would have been to run inside to my bed and hide under the covers but I was frozen still. I was sure at first, it was Tommy, but he didn't have a face. It seemed like he waved for me to come closer but that is when I really became scared and I ran into the house.

I was too afraid to be alone so I crawled into bed next to Jimmy. This scared me more than the other things that I have seen because I know this time it wasn't a dream. It took a while to get to sleep but I finally did.

Jimmy woke me up in the morning. "Another bad dream huh?" He asked. "No. This was worse." I said and then I told him what happened. He tried to make sense out of it and he told me that I was probably sleep walking or the fog was playing tricks on my eyes. I know he believed me. He just didn't want it to scare him also.

When we got downstairs to the breakfast table Dad and Mom had strange looks on their faces. "Which one of you guys were playing around in the shed yesterday?" Dad asked. Jimmy and me looked at each other and we were speechless. "Next time you go in there remember to close the doors." Dad said. "You boys know better than that. One other thing Stevie." Mom said. "Yes Mom?" I replied. "What is the name of the priest that you have been talking to lately?" She asked "Father O'Reilly. Why? I asked. "That's what I was afraid of." Mom said as she handed me the morning paper and pointed to an article. It said:

Father Joseph O'Reilly of the St. Peters Clergy was reported missing yesterday. Father O'Reilly has been a member of St. Peters for the last seventeen years...

The article went on. "I can't believe this. What is going on?" I asked. "We can't believe it either. We are going to be taking some extra security measures until some sense is made out of all of the things that have been occurring around here. From now on I am driving you guys to school myself and we are not letting you out of our sight in the afternoons and weekends." Dad said.

The only thing I could think of all day at school was Father O'Reilly. What could've happened to him? I couldn't even go to the church by myself anymore. How was I going to talk to Tommy? Maybe I could meet him by the shed. I wasn't really sure if that was him though. I was just so confused over all of the strange things that were going on. I just couldn't wait to talk to Mike again. He really understood what I was feeling. I hoped everything was okay with him.

The Cray's were just getting comfortable at their Motel. Teddy and Rachel were splashing around in the pool and Mr. and Mrs. Cray were sipping their cocktails by the Tiki bar overlooking them. They were talking with the bartender and some other Motel guests. They all told each other where they were from and what they did for a living.

Mr. Cray made it clear that he wasn't there to talk shop but deep down inside it was all that he could think of. The Cray's didn't say a word to the others about any of the strange goings on that they have been a part of recently. They just wanted to fit in and have a good time.

Teddy and Rachel met some other kids their age that were staying with their parents at the Motel too. It seemed like a perfect getaway for the family.

After school I was sitting in the living room watching television as my Dad walked in from work.

"Hello everyone. I have a surprise, look who I found." Dad said. Eddie walked in behind him. "Eddie! Hi, it's great to see you!" Mom said as she gave him a hug and a kiss. "It's great to see you too!" Eddie replied.

Eddie still didn't look like his fun self. I guess he was still upset about Mrs. Stages. Mom spoke to her a couple of days ago and she told Dad that she didn't sound so hot either.

"Hey Eddie. What's happening?" I asked. "I'm good little man. What's new with you?" Eddie replied. "I'm doing fine." I said. "Mike is going to come by in a little while to watch the game with us. You and your Brother could join us if you want." Dad said.

After we all ate dinner Mike knocked on the door. "Hello all." Mike said. "Hey, come on in." Dad said. Mike talked to Dad, Mom and Eddie for a little while before he came into the den.

"Hey dream kid. What's going on?" Mike asked as he walked into the den. "Hi Mike, too much going on with me." I replied. "I heard. I'm sorry about Father O'Reilly." Mike said. "Thanks, I don't understand why." I told Mike. Mike explained to me that a lot of things that go on in this world can't be explained and we have to hope and pray for the best.

Even though he didn't say too much about it, it always makes me feel better just having Mike around. I filled him in on what I seen by the shed the night before. He told me that I am always able to top myself. I realized that too after he mentioned it. We talked about that for a while before Dad, Eddie and Jimmy came in to watch the game with us.

Billy was over at O'Kelly's talking with Brian the bartender. He filled Brian in on his date with Donna the night before. "How far did you get? Or did you forget how to do that stuff?" Brian asked. "I didn't forget anything. In fact, I was pretty damn good." Billy replied.

"Billy, Billy, you'll never guess. Hi Brian. You'll never guess who that car is registered to." Bob said as he ran toward Billy. "Who? Who?" Billy asked. "Tell the owl." Brian joked. "Do you remember the name Muekaz?" Bob asked. "Muekaz? Muekaz? Oh shit! Yea, from the apartment." Billy said. "Yep, and that's exactly where his address came up as." Bob said.

"Isn't that some shit? Oh shit, wait a second. Donna! That guy knows where she lives now." Billy said as he grabbed Brian's phone and dialed Donna's number. "Hello" Donna said. "Oh thank God! It's me, Billy." Billy said. "Oh, how nice, they usually don't call the night after." Donna said. "Good one. You want to hear more police talk? I have to get you the hell out of that house. I will explain when I get there. Just put on something sexy and I'll be there in about fifteen minutes." Billy said. "Okay but why do I have to put on something sexy?" Donna asked. "Why not?" Billy replied as he hung up and ran out to his car. "Ahhh, young love." Brian said. Bob raised his glass. "To young love!" He said.

The next morning Billy woke up next to Donna at his apartment. He explained the whole Muekaz situation to her the night before. He told her that he had to get to work and that she should stay at his place or stay with a family member until this case is closed. She decided that she should stay with her friend Tina. Billy thought that was a good idea and he told her to get dressed so he could drop her off there on his way to work.

When Billy dropped Donna off Tina came out to say hi. "How have you been handsome? How's your cute friend Eddie?" Tina asked. "He's still as cute as a button." Billy joked. "Why don't you tell him that we are all ready for that double date?" Tina asked. "I certainly will, and you look out for this little lady. Here is my number at the precinct. Call me if anything happens." Billy said as he kissed Donna goodbye.

I just finished my breakfast and I asked Mom if she could take me to the church. It had been a while since I had been there, so I was anxious to get back. Mom told me that it would be fine but we couldn't stay too long. She had a lot of things to do. In between food shopping and other things we were able to stop by the church. I quickly found a quiet place where I could share my feelings with Tommy. My Mother ended up talking to a Nun about Father O'Reilly.

The Nun told Mom all of the great details about Father O'Reilly and she also told Mom that he would be back. She said that he would be found soon. Mom was happy to hear that, although she doesn't know how the Nun knows this. Mom said that the Nun was absolutely positive.

I didn't see the Nun. I was busy having a word with Tommy. Tommy didn't verify whether or not it was him at the shed but he did tell me to make Rachel stop. He said that she shouldn't play around with things that she is not sure of. I had no idea what he meant by that but I assured him that she would get his message as soon as I seen her.

Mom rushed me out. She had to get home. On the way home she went on and on about how Sister Taryas made her feel so confident about Father O'Reilly and how she could swear that she knew her voice from somewhere. We were home before two o'clock. Mom was in a hurry because she wanted to have dinner ready early so that she could do some things around the house. She usually does that on Sunday afternoons. She always says, before you know it, it's Monday morning.

Mom was right, before I knew it; I was back in school Monday morning. I was feeling a little jealous of Teddy and Rachel; they were still on vacation. I was two hours into my school day and they were just waking up to go for a swim.

Rachel met with one of the other girls that were staying at the Motel. Her name is Danielle. Rachel and Danielle got to know each other pretty well over the last couple of days. Rachel didn't tell her about what had recently happened to her but she did share her interest in the unexplained. "That stuff interests me too. My only problem with it is, when I hear too much about it, it scares me and I can't go to sleep. One time my cousin told me about a haunted house on her block where an old man died and I couldn't sleep for almost a week. So you know I'm having a really hard time sleeping in this Motel." Danielle said.

"Why can't you sleep here? Do you miss your bed?" Rachel asked. "Duh, how am I supposed to sleep in a haunted Motel?" Danielle asked. "What do you mean haunted?" Rachel asked. "You got to be kidding me. You didn't hear the sounds over the last couple of nights? I slept on the floor next to my parent's bed

133

with my pillow over my head all night. This place is known for being haunted." Danielle went on. Rachel's eyes lit up. This is right up her alley. "You're serious? I wasn't able to hear anything, maybe because I have so much on my mind. If this is true, I want some proof. Do you want to hang out tonight and experiment? Rachel asked.

"I am willing to under one condition, the other guys have to come too. I would be too scared if it was just the two of us." Danielle said. "That sounds okay with me. I'll get my Brother and we'll see if Timmy and Joey want to come too." Rachel said. They agreed and decided to find the boys after their swim.

Mr. and Mrs. Cray were just waking up. They had a late night with the other parents. They were having a really great time away from their troubles at home. Mr. Cray threw on a pair of sweat pants. "Honey, I'm going to get some coffee. Do you want anything else?" He asked. "Coffee is fine. We have orange juice in the fridge also." Mrs. Cray said.

Mr. Cray ran into one of the other guys from the night before. He was also getting coffee. "Hey Doc, good morning." Mr. Cray said. "Good morning officer. How are you feeling?" Doc asked. Mr. Cray called him Doc because he didn't remember his name but he knew that he was a Doctor. "Feeling good, I'll feel even better after some coffee. I had a great time last night. How about you?" Mr. Cray asked. "The best. Are we on again for tonight? This is your last night here, right?" Doc asked. "Yes and yes. Tonight will be even better." Mr. Cray said. "We'll see you at the bar at around seven." Doc said as they both walked back to their rooms.

"Here you go, cream and two sugars, sugar." Mr. Cray said as he handed a coffee to Mrs. Cray. "Oh how sweet." Mrs. Cray replied. "Where are those kids? Out already? It's nice that there are kids here their age to keep them busy." Mr. Cray said. "Yea, who would've expected everything to work out so perfect? Mrs. Cray said.

Mr. Cray got himself together and decided to get in a workout at the Motel gym before lunch. Mrs. Cray was going to play some tennis with a couple of the ladies she met at the Motel. None of them were pro's but they figured why not try it out since the courts were there.

Later on, back at home, Billy just got off of his shift and arrived at his apartment. He just finished speaking with Dad about Eddie. Billy was getting Eddie's phone number and he wanted to find out from Dad if Eddie had any interest in Tina. Dad told him that it would probably be a really good idea for Eddie to hang out with Tina. Dad figured that would get Mrs. Stages off of Eddie's mind.

Eddie's phone rang and he picked it up. "Hello." Eddie said. "Hey Eddie. How's it going? It's Bill." Billy said. "Hey, what a surprise, not much going on here. What's new with you? Eddie asked. "I got an extra ticket to the ballet and I wanted to see if you were busy or not." Billy joked. They both laughed. "Seriously, do you remember Tina?" Billy asked, "Oh, how could I forget Tina?" Eddie replied "Well, she is still very interested in you and she wanted to see if you wanted to get together with her, Donna and me." Billy said. "I don't know, uhmmm." Eddie paused. "No, wait, you know what? I think that's a great idea."

Eddie said. "I'm glad to hear that. How does Saturday sound for you?" Billy asked. "Saturday sounds perfect. Why don't you give me a call Friday afternoon and we'll plan the whole thing?" Eddie suggested. "Great. I'll talk to you then." Billy said and they hung up.

Chapter XIII

Back at my house, Dad and Mom were talking. "It looks like good old Billy found something to get Karen off of Eddie's mind." Dad said. "Oh yea? What's that?" Mom asked. "Remember that girl from the bar that caused this whole mess?" Dad asked. "Oh yea, how could I forget?" What a day that was." Mom replied. "Well, Billy is dating that girls friend and they are setting up a double date." Dad said. "Well, it's not a bad idea to get Eddie back to normal but I think he could do much better than that girl." Mom said. "I guess she is a little sleazy but it's just for fun. I don't think they're going to get engaged. Young guys need a tramp like that every once in a while." Dad joked and Mom smirked. "Real cute mister. I am not going to get involved. I learned my lesson about match making." Mom said. "Your heart was in the right place, besides, I don't think these two are going to last too long anyway. What is that kid up to now?" Dad asked as he looked out the back window and seen me in the shed.

I was looking through the shed wondering if I would feel a vibe from Tommy. I made sure I went out there before the sun went down. I didn't want to go near that shed in the dark. I was out there for about a half-hour just waiting for some kind of a sign from Tommy. Nothing was happening so I decided to go back into the house. I made sure that I shut the doors of the shed, just in case it was my fault last time.

Back at the Motel, the Cray's were just finishing up their dinner. They were at a small restaurant down the road from the Motel. "Can I get you anything else?" The waitress asked. "I can't fit another thing. How about you guys? Mr. Cray asked. "No thank you. I'm stuffed." Mrs. Cray replied, and Teddy and Rachel agreed.

"So, you guys are here on vacation?" The waitress asked. "Yep, this is our last night here." Mr. Cray said. "Oh, where are you staying?" The waitress asked. "Right down the road at Murry's Inn." Mr. Cray said. "Oh, so you guys don't scare too easy." The waitress said. "How's that?" Mr. Cray asked. "The haunted Murry's Inn. Anyone who stays there has to be fearless. It scares me just to be working this close to that place." The waitress said. "We really had no idea. Teddy, why don't you take your Sister to see the horses outside?" Mr. Cray suggested. "Yea, that's a good idea and don't get too close to them." Mrs. Cray said. "Cool, let's go Rache." Teddy said.

Teddy and Rachel got up and ran towards the farm behind the restaurant. Mr. and Mrs. Cray could see them from the window. "So, what's the story with this Motel?" Mr. Cray asked. The waitress sat down. "Well, it goes back about fifteen years. Back then there was a traveler who stayed there for a night by himself. There was also a family of four in another room and a young couple in another. Those were the only occupied rooms for the night. Murry had to run out and take care of some things at his other place. He left the handyman, Jedly there by himself to look after things. Jedly was kind of slow but he seemed harmless. Later that night the family of four and the young couple swore that they heard screams and knocks on their walls throughout the whole night. The man of the family told reporters the next day that every time he heard a knock, he went to check it out and there wasn't anyone around any of the times. He said that there wasn't anyone staying in the room next to his. He stared out of the window into the next room until he heard the next bang. It was louder than the earlier ones and it was followed by a high-pitched scream. That's when he decided to gather his family, pack the car and get out of there. He said as they pulled out of the parking lot his wife looked into their room from the car and she seen the ceiling lamp swaying back and forth and flickering. She also saw the door opening slowly. After that, they just sped away and they didn't want to ever see that place again. The police tracked them down the next morning." The waitress said.

"Holy shit, that is weird. A few weeks ago I would've said, that is a bunch of nonsense but I recently had an eye opening experience." Mr. Cray said. "What about the other couple and the man?" Mrs. Cray asked. "Well, the couple was also questioned. The man said that he couldn't sleep, he was up watching television while his girlfriend was sleeping. As soon as he started to doze off, he looked to his right and next to the bed he saw the outline of a figure. Not a person, just an outline. He said as soon as he saw that, he yelled and jumped on top of his girlfriend to protect her and at the same time he scared the shit out of her. They had a rough time falling back to sleep after that. The man didn't tell his girlfriend what he seen until the morning. After he told her is when she told him about her dream. She was dreaming that her boyfriend was getting up to get a closer look at something across the room and at the exact moment in her dream when he got to what he was looking at is when he jumped on her. The thing in the dream that the boyfriend was getting a closer look at was his Father in a coffin." The waitress said.

"Oh my God. I won't be able to sleep tonight." Mrs. Cray said. "What about Jedly, the handyman and the other guy?" Mr. Cray asked. "That's the reason why the police were involved. Those two were never accounted for. No one has seen them since." The waitress said. "Holy shit. That's too much." Mr. Cray said.

"That's just how it started. So many other things have happened there since then. Just last week a couple left there screaming their heads off, saying that they are not paying for their stay and that they are going to take Murry to court. They said that they actually seen something floating across their room." The waitress said.

"So honey, are you ready to go back and get a good nights sleep?" Mr. Cray asked. "I am ready to get to the bar." Mrs. Cray replied. "I'm sorry, I hope I didn't disrupt your vacation." The waitress said. "Oh no, you supplied some great conversation to share with the other couples at the bar." Mr. Cray said. They said goodnight to the waitress and got Teddy and Rachel.

Mr. and Mrs. Cray were surprised that Teddy and Rachel didn't question what the waitress said. They just figured that they forgot. They didn't know that Teddy and Rachel had plans to experiment with the haunted Motel. Now the kids had more proof that it was haunted.

At seven thirty the kids all met up by the pool and Mr. and Mrs. Cray went to the outdoor Motel bar and met up with the other parents. The kids went over to the bar to let their parents know that they would be in the game room downstairs.

When they got down to the game room it was very dark and most of the games were out of order. They weren't planning on playing them anyway. Rachel brought a candle; she lit it and placed it on one of the game tables. Joey took out a rectangular piece of cardboard and a magic marker. "What are you going to do with that?" Teddy asked. "This is how you make a home made Ouija board." Joey said. Joey sat down and started writing on the cardboard.

"That's not gonna work." Timmy said. "It will, I know people that do it like this. They say it's better than the real thing." Joey said with confidence. "Real or fake, I'm not touching that thing. It's evil, I'll just sit here and watch you maniacs." Timmy said.

Joey finished preparing his homemade Ouija board and the others were very impressed by it. They sat down to get started. "If there are any spirits in this Motel, show us a sign!" Joey yelled out. After a pause Timmy shook his head. "I told you, nothing is going to" Timmy was cut short as a loud bang came from the next room. They all froze up and had frightened looks on their faces, except for Joey. "I guess I got someone's attention." Joey said. It was a good thing that Joey was there, he made it a little less scary for the rest of them. Even with all of their fear, they decided to continue.

Joey, Rachel, Danielle and Teddy put their hands on the board. "Who are you?" Joey asked. After a long pause their hands were brought to the letter J. Next they were slowly brought to the letter E. It started to speed up a bit and went to D. After that it followed up with an L and then a Y. Then it stopped. "Jedly? Who the hell is Jedly?" Joey asked.

After a long pause it went to S. Next it went to T, then it sped up and went to O and then P. "We better stop." Joey said sarcastically. Next it brought them to I, then S. Next it went to A, followed by I and D. "I said? What did I said?" Joey asked. Then it spelled out S.T.O.P again. They were all getting a little nervous. After a couple of minutes it spelled out R.A.C.H.E.L. "Rachel, I think Jedly wants you to stop, if it's still Jedly. Is this still Jedly? Joey asked. It sped over to the corner to NO. Then it spelled out T.O.M.M.Y. "Oh no." Rachel said. "I think you mean Timmy." Joey said.

Timmy looked like he was ready to cry. It went back to NO again and then it spelled out S.T.A.G.E.S. Teddy and Rachel let go. "We can't do this anymore." Teddy said. "Why not?" Joey asked and then another loud bang came from the next room. Timmy ran out of the room. Joey ran out to stop him. "He is going to get us all in trouble." Joey said as he chased after him. "Who is Tommy Stages?" Danielle asked. "He was a friend of ours that died recently." Teddy said. "I can't believe this." Rachel said. "I think we should let this go Rache." Teddy said.

"Let's just see if he could tell us what has been going on in the neighborhood." Rachel said as Joey came back in with Timmy. "That's not a good idea Rache, he said stop." Teddy said. Rachel touched the board and then there was a long disturbing roar that sounded like a plane landing in the Motel. They all got up and ran out.

All of the parents at the bar got up off of their stools. "Let me go check, if there is any trouble over there it has to be our sweet little Joey." Doc said as he walked toward where the noise came from.

The kids calmed down and walked out of the Motel. "What are you guys up to?" Doc asked. "We didn't do anything wrong Dad. That loud bang just scared us out of the game room. Did you hear it?" Joey asked. "Yes, we all heard it. Why don't you guys go play nicely over by the swings?" Doc suggested.

Doc went back to the bar and Mr. and Mrs. Cray felt that it was a perfect time to bring up what the waitress told them. Doc and his wife were surprised but everyone else knew about the Motel being haunted. The bartender confirmed the stories and shared some other ones. He told everyone how it has been exceptionally quiet this past week. He told them that normally you would be seeing lights and TV's flickering and hearing all sorts of noises like the one they just heard.

"About a month ago, I was out here cleaning up. It was very late; a guest came running over here and ordered a bottle of Vodka. I told him that I don't usually sell it by the bottle and I asked him what was wrong. He told me that he thinks he is seeing and hearing things. His wife was asleep and he didn't want to disturb her with his imagination. I told him that it's probably not his imagination and I asked him what he saw. He told me that he was sitting up in bed watching the TV and it went off by itself. He got up and turned it back on and from where he was standing he could see into the room across the way. There was nobody staying in that room. He noticed the light go on over there. He walked closer to the window and he seen the shades move in the window. He said that his body was overwhelmed with heat at that point and he heard something behind him. He quickly turned around and he saw a flash, something moved across his room. He said that he knew it wasn't a person or an animal because of the way it moved. He turned around again and he seen the light go off in the other room. That's when he noticed me out here cleaning up and he decided he needed a strong drink. When he headed to the door to come over here the TV shut off again. He wanted to bring the bottle back with him but he ended up drinking most of it out here with me. I told him about this crazy place. He was just happy to know that he wasn't losing his mind. I am pretty used to this stuff. I have been working here for years. One of the freakiest stories though, has to be when four nuns stayed here about twelve years ago. Supposedly they were on their way back from a retreat and the van driver was getting tired so he asked them if it would be okay if they stopped for the night. The nuns decided it was a good idea, but as it turned out it was a very bad idea. They left very early in the morning, just after a couple of minutes on the highway; they were struck by a tractor-trailer. All four of the nuns, and the van driver died. It was very sad. If they would have drove through the night they would probably all still be alive. Nobody knows if it had anything to do with religious people staying in a demonic Motel, but there are a lot of people that are quick to make that connection." The bartender said. "I think we could all use a refill." Mr. Cray said.

The parents stayed at the bar till very late that night. They had to have some fear of going to those haunted rooms after all of the stories they were sharing. The kids ended up falling asleep after talking in the playground. The parents carried them back to their rooms later on. None of them were able to get a good night sleep. The Motel seemed to have extra creeks and noises that night.

At around five AM everyone was woken up by screams coming from the game room. Doc got out of his bed and checked on Timmy and Joey. Timmy was there but Joey was missing. The parents scattered to find him. They followed the screams into the game room. The door was locked but it was just a frail piece of wood with some hinges. Doc broke it down and discovered his son Joey screaming in his sleep with his home made Ouija board next to him.

Doc woke Joey up. Joey was hysterical crying. Doc carried him back to his room. Mr. Cray with his police instinct picked up the Ouija board and brought it back to the room to question Teddy and Rachel.

Joey was okay, he was just frightened. He told his parents that he had a horrible nightmare and they figured that he was sleep walking and ended up in the game room.

Teddy and Rachel told Mr. Cray what they did and he was very disappointed with them. He was also a bit shocked when they told him that someone named Jedly spoke to them. Mr. Cray felt like he was being tested. "I went from a non believer into Mr. afterlife in less than a week. I think we enjoyed the hell out of our vacation but someone is telling us to end it while we can. Everyone get your stuff together, we are leaving here the same way many others have left here. Fast and in the middle of the night." Mr. Cray said. They packed quickly and said goodbye to Doc and whoever else was awake at the time. The Cray's caught up on their sleep at home most of Tuesday.

Chapter XIV

Wednesday before Mr. Cray went back to work he called Mike. Mike was the first one he wanted to talk to about what went on. Mr. Cray feels the same way about Mike that I do. He knows that Mike is the best one to talk to about things like this. They decided to meet after Mr. Cray's shift for a drink at O'Kelly's.

Mr. Cray filled Mike in on all of the details of his haunted vacation. "Between you and Stevie, I don't know how I am supposed to sleep at night. Your stories get stranger and stranger. You must have been scared shitless. I feel like I am surrounded by nightmares and horror movies. If I shared all of these details with Sarah she would never be able to go to sleep again." Mike said.

"I know. It is really insane. Do you think that it has anything to do with Jerry and Tommy?" Mr. Cray asked. "I think it has all to do with them. They are the main source of Stevie's dreams. Whenever he tells me about his dreams they normally involve one or the other or both of them. Speaking of Stevie, did you hear about his friend the priest?" Mike asked. "No, what?" Mr. Cray asked. "He was the latest to be reported as missing." Mike informed Mr. Cray. "No shit? What the hell is going on around here?" Mr. Cray asked. "Oh before I forget, I have something new to add to the puzzle, read this." Mike said as he handed Mr. Cray the letter written by Stacey Riches. Mr. Cray read it.

147

> After they visit the third floor, the dog
> will find the body that you buried in the
> shed. You're not going to be able to
> stop the information obtainer.
> Your friends can cast stones or spread
> flames but that will not even any score.
> Billy won't let you get away with it.
> You can't hide your K D L forever.

"Where did this come from? Mr. Cray asked. "Do you remember that singer girl Stacey that I was supposed to protect while she was in town?" Mike asked. "Yea, the one in the accident. She wrote this?" Mr. Cray asked. "Yes, she had some strange encounters a while back of her own." Mike said as he explained the night in the hospital of when Stacey clinically died. Mr. Cray was amazed by the story. Mike didn't share the story with Mr. Cray earlier because that was when Mr. Cray thought all of that stuff was nonsense.

"Keep it down, you are going to scare off all of my customers." Brian said as he walked towards the guys. "Don't worry about us, your customers scare each other away." Mr. Cray said as he nodded toward Mr. Glacey. "I'm noter scareded of nanyone." Mr. Glacey chimed in.

"Welcome back old timer." Billy said as he entered the bar. "The towns been a wreck without ya!" Bob yelled as he followed Billy in. The guys all shook hands and hugged. "How was the trip?" Billy asked. "Beautiful, I want to get away more often." Mr. Cray said. "Except for the." Mike started to say as Mr. Cray cut him off. Mr. Cray didn't want Bob and Billy to know about what happened at the Motel.

"We may have some kind of lead on something. Who the hell knows what?" Bob said. "What the hell does that mean?" Mr. Cray asked. "Well, do you remember the Muekaz character from the apartment with the dead guy in the shed? Billy asked. "Sure I do. "Mr. Cray replied. "It seems he was tailing me the other night." Billy said. The guys informed Ted about the license plates and Billy's trip that night.

"This Muekaz guy is acting like he has some score to settle but we can't make any connection." Bob said. "Do you think he may have something to do with the fire at the poker game or the brick through the window?" Mr. Cray asked. "I really didn't make that connection but it does make sense." Billy said. "And you're supposed to be a cop?" Mr. Cray said as the guys laughed. "That son of a bitch owes me a new window!" Brian exclaimed. "Lets not assume too quickly." Mr. Cray said. "But you just said" Billy said as Mr. Cray motioned to Mike to let him see the note from Stacey Riches once again. Mr. Cray read it to himself again. "May I?" Mr. Cray asked Mike as he folded the paper and placed it in his inside jacket pocket. "Sure, I guess. Just don't lose it." Mike replied.

Bob and Billy didn't know what that was about. They were talking to Brian and ordering beers. Mr. Cray took a deeper interest in Muekaz. After Rachel's kidnapping the guys tried to find whatever they could on him but they couldn't come up with anything. Mr. Cray believed that there has to be something somewhere with this guy's name on it. The guys sat there till late at night discussing Muekaz.

Back at my house, it had to be about three in the morning when I was awakened by yet another strange dream. I was walking around a pond in complete darkness when a man started to walk towards me. I was very scared. The man stopped in front of me and a light shined on him. It was Mr. Stages. He said hello to me and told me to relax. I couldn't speak. He told me that he has a mission for me. I just nodded "Yes." He told me that I must meet Eddie at this pond on Saturday at noon to give him some information. I still couldn't speak to ask him what the information was. Mr. Stages said not to worry. He said that I would be given the information before I get there. He just told me to make sure I call Eddie and give him these directions and tell him Saturday at noon. Again I nodded "Yes." After he was sure that I understood, he gave me another message. He said that Tommy told Rachel to stop on the Ouija board because Tommy was trying to make sure that the Motel was calmer than normal while the Cray's stayed there. He also wanted her to know that she was getting involved in something that she didn't belong. The spirits in the Motel are known to attach themselves to guests that play games with them. Joey's life will change from his sarcasm. That Motel is infested with evil spirits. There are peaceful spirits and evil spirits, that Motel contains only evil.

After my dream, I wrote down the directions to the pond and everything else that Mr. Stages told me. It took a while but I eventually fell back to sleep.

In the morning I came down to the breakfast table and asked Dad if he was going to be talking to Eddie before Saturday. "I will probably see him tomorrow, why do you ask?" Dad asked. "There is something I have to talk to him about. It's kind of another dream thing." I said. "Whatever I could do to help, just let me know Stevie." Dad said. "When you talk to him tomorrow could you drop something off to him for me?" I asked. "Sure, not a problem." Dad replied. "That would be great. Thanks Dad." I said.

Dad dropped Jimmy and me off at our schools and he headed to work. While I was at school Rachel was seeing Gary, her psychologist. This was only her second visit but she became very comfortable with him. Gary knew that she had been through something traumatic but he didn't know the whole story. He asked Rachel for some information about the day she was taken away. She informed him of the details of what led up to her kidnapping. She explained that she had been lurking around her Uncle Vinny's apartment. She told him that she was interested in the paranormal activities that have been said to be taking place over there. "I was walking through the rooms and I heard some noise coming from the back of the apartment. I went back there to see what it was. I saw two men in there taking things apart. I turned around to run and one of the men grabbed me. He twisted my arm behind my back and knocked me down. After that everything became a blur. I can recall being taken away in a van with my arms and legs tied." Rachel explained.

Gary listened closely and took notes. He acted as if it wasn't so bad, just so she wouldn't get nervous. Inside he couldn't believe the story. "Well, you have been through a lot young lady. May I say that it looks like you are handling it great? That is very important."

Gary told Rachel and they discussed the event thoroughly.

When Rachel was about to bring up her experience at the haunted Motel, Gary informed her that their hour was up and that he would like to continue in one week. He did ask her if there was anything else that she needed to say but she figured that could wait a week.

Gary brought Rachel out to the waiting room where Mrs. Cray was sitting. Rachel noticed David Stoub sitting in the other waiting room with a magazine in front of his face. David is the kid that my Brother Jimmy almost had a fight with. David didn't see Rachel walk by.

Gary told Mrs. Cray that Rachel is handling everything very good. He also informed her to listen to her Daughter whenever she needs to talk about anything. "She is the only one that could tell you what she has been through. Doctor, Patient confidentiality, you understand? I would like to see her again in one week if that is okay with you." Gary said. "That should be fine but how about after school? She should be back to class by then." Mrs. Cray said. "That should be fine. Is four o'clock good?" Gary asked. "That would be perfect. See you then and thank you for everything." Mrs. Cray said as they left.

When they got to the car Rachel told her Mother that she left something in Gary's office and she had to run back in. She went to Gary's office door and put her ear up against it. She heard David speaking about his life at home. She knew that she shouldn't be listening to other people's sessions, but that is how she is. She was known for eavesdropping.

Rachel went back to the car and her Mother took her out for lunch. Mrs. Cray hinted to Rachel that if she needs to talk about anything, she would always be there. Rachel thanked her but she didn't want to talk to anyone about what happened except for Gary.

After their lunch they stopped over at my house. Mrs. Cray wanted to see Mom. They haven't had a chance to talk about things for a while. While they were talking I came in from school. One of my classmates Fathers dropped me off. Since so many strange things have been going on in the neighborhood, the parents arranged a car-pooling system. I greeted Mom and Mrs. Cray. After we talked for a little bit they told me that Rachel was in the other room watching TV.

"Hey, how are you feeling?" I asked Rachel. "Hi. I'm good. How about you? I haven't seen you in a while." Rachel said. After we caught up with each other I started to tell her about how Tommy wanted me to warn her about messing around with stuff that she shouldn't be. "Are you serious? Why the heck couldn't you tell me that before we went on vacation? You could've saved me a big scare. Do you know what happened at that Motel?" Rachel asked, as she was about to tell me about the Ouija board and Joey. "As a matter of fact, I do have an idea of what happened." I said as I began telling her what Mr. Stages told me in the dream. I also showed her what I wrote after the dream.

Rachel was amazed. "You even have Joey's name written down. Now I have to believe you. What happened to Joey? Did Mr. Stages tell you anything about that?" Rachel asked. "No, he just said that things are different in his life now." I said.

"What is all of this other stuff about? A pond and Eddie?" Rachel asked. "Don't worry about that, that is something I have to work out with somebody else. You should just worry about listening to what Tommy tells you." I told Rachel. "Believe me, I am finished playing with that kind of stuff." Rachel said. After that she told me everything that went on in the haunted Motel.

The next day was Friday. I was anxious to get home from school to find out if Dad was able to drop off my note and directions to the pond for Eddie.

Eddie was on the phone with Billy making their plans for their big double date with Tina and Donna. They decided to have Billy pick up the girls and then meet by Eddie's for a few drinks before they go out for dinner. They agreed to meet at Eddie's at five o'clock.

A short while after Eddie hung up with Billy, he called Dad at work. They talked for a while. Dad asked Eddie if he knew about Rachel coming home. "Rachel, you've come, back!" Eddie replied with his impression of Jackie Gleason. They both laughed and Dad informed him that he had something to drop off to him from me. Dad also told Eddie that he is supposed to meet me on Saturday. Dad explained to him that it had to do with one of my famous dreams. "Sure, I don't have a problem with doing any favors for that kid. Whatever he needs, he got it." Eddie said. "Great, I'll stop by on my way home and drop off the papers that he wrote for you." Dad said.

"Do you know what it is all about?" Eddie asked. "I think it's the recipe for no-cal pizza or the directions to the warehouse that holds two thousand handy housewife helpers." Dad joked. He was quoting another episode of The Honeymooners. "If it's not one crazy hair brain scheme, it's another." Eddie joked back. "Funny Alice, you're a regular riot, but seriously, I don't know what it's all about. I am not invading Stevie's privacy by reading it either. That is between you and him. I'll be out of here in a little while, I'll see you when I get there." Dad said.

Dad got to Eddies a short while later and dropped of my note and directions. When Dad drove away, Eddie opened the note and read it.

> Hi Eddie, I am anxious to find out what this is all about too. I had a dream the other night and I received an important message from Mr. Stages. He wants you to follow the attached directions and meet me at this pond Saturday at noon. I don't know why the day and time are so important. I also don't really know what I am going to be giving you yet, but he told me that he would let me know before I get there. Please just be there. He made it sound like it is very important, like life and death. You know how my dreams have been giving really strong messages lately. That's the only reason I am interrupting your schedule. Meet me at the spot where I marked the X. I will be there at noon on Saturday.

> Thank you very much, Stevie.

Eddie finished reading the letter and became very nervous. He had hundreds of thoughts running through his mind. He is sure that Mr. Stages is unhappy with him because of his interest in Mrs. Stages. His main worry is that he might receive some kind of warning to stay away from her. The part about life and death stuck in his mind. Eddie knows how real my dreams are and that scared him even more.

When Dad got home he assured me that my message was delivered successfully and that Eddie would definitely be happy to help me any way he could. I am so relieved that the first part of my mission had been pulled off. I explained most of what was going on to Dad. He insisted that he would drive me to the pond because of all of the occurrences in our town lately. Now Dad is feeling nervous too. He also thinks that Mr. Stages is angry with Eddie.

Eddie was up all night worried about what was going to happen to him. Dad was also having difficulty sleeping because of it. I was just anxious, wondering how Mr. Stages was going to give me whatever it was that he was supposed to give me.

When the morning arrived I was a little disappointed because I didn't have any dreams that I could remember. I thought for sure that my message would come in my dream. I rushed through my breakfast and everything else I had to do. I carried the directions with me everywhere I went throughout the house. I helped Dad outside with some yard work. We were out front and Dad asked me to get a small shovel from the shed in the back. I ran to the yard and thought that maybe my message would be in the shed. I went in and looked around for the small shovel. I couldn't find it. I put the directions down on a shelf and I started to move things around. Finally I found the shovel and I ran back to give it to Dad. We continued the yard work, as it got closer to noon. "Let's wrap up here, it's almost time to go on your adventure." Dad said.

We got cleaned up and we were all set to go. We got into the car. "Okay, I'm going to need those directions buddy." Dad said. I looked through my pockets. "Oh no, I left them on the shelf in the shed. I'll be right back." I told Dad.

I went to the shelf where I left the paper and it was gone. I looked all over in the shed and I couldn't find it anywhere. I checked my pockets again and there was nothing. I went back to the car to let Dad know that I couldn't find the paper. Dad got out of the car and we both looked. We couldn't find it anywhere. "Do you think you could find this place by memory?" Dad asked. "I guess I could. That's the way I did it last time." I said.

At a few minutes passed twelve, Eddie was sitting on a bench by the pond waiting for me. He was a nervous wreck and shaking. He just finished pacing and he decided to have a seat. A little while later, he glanced over his left shoulder and he caught a glimpse of something. Eddie could not believe his eyes. He turned around and stood up. He started to shake even more.

The message that I was supposed to bring got there without me. It was Mrs. Stages standing in front of Eddie with tears in her eyes. The two of them stared at each other for a moment and then stepped closer and embraced. That is when Dad and me finally pulled up.

We realized that the paper disappeared for a reason. That must have been the message that Mr. Stages told me about.

Mrs. Stages was crying her eyes out. She was at the pond in the middle of telling Mr. Stages that she is at the end of her rope. She told him that she goes to that pond at least once a week so that he would hopefully give her a reason to carry on. She was also telling him that this would be her last visit to the pond. She told him that she was ready to join her dead husband and son. She was about to walk away from the pond to go home to overdose on sleeping pills. That also turned out to be the reason that Tommy made me visit his Mother the day he gave me that strong feeling. She was considering overdosing then also. That wasn't candy that I heard hitting the floor that day.

As she told Mr. Stages that she needed a sign from him not to go through with it is when she glanced over her right shoulder and seen Eddie sitting there.

Dad reached over to shake my hand. "Another job well done son." Dad said. "Thanks Dad." I replied. "Now let's get out of here before these love birds see us." Dad said as we pulled away. We headed over to Lenny's for an ice cream celebration.

Eddie and Mrs. Stages hung around by the pond and talked for a couple of hours. They told each other what made them go to the pond. Mrs. Stages was completely amazed by my dream. Eddie also shared the letter with her.

After that, they went to a diner for a late lunch. When they finished eating it was almost five o'clock. "Would you like to stop by my house quickly so I could clean myself up? Eddie asked. "That would be fine." Mrs. Stages replied. At that moment Eddie looked across the street and noticed a man coming out of an office building. "I know that guy. Holy shit, it's Tightass!" Eddie exclaimed. "The guy that tried to frame you at your job?" Mrs. Stages asked. "You got it. I have to call someone, or first we have to follow him to see where he goes." Eddie said in a nervous state.

Eddie and Mrs. Stages followed Tightass to a Motel. Eddie waited to see which room he went into and then quickly got to a pay phone. "Who should I call? Who should I call? A cop. Yea a cop, I guess I should call a cop. Oh shit, it's five o'clock, there's a cop at my house." Eddie thought to himself.

That is when Eddie realized that seeing Tightass was the best thing that could happen to him at this moment. Eddie was about to bring Mrs. Stages back to his house. They would have run into Billy and the girls. That would have been a complete mess. "Thank you Tightass, you saved my ass." Eddie thought to himself.

Eddie called Dad to inform him of what was going on. "You old dog. I told you Stevie's dreams are something to take seriously." Dad said. "You couldn't be more right. I can't begin to tell you how shocked I am about that, and equally happy. There is something else I have to tell you about right now." Eddie said. "Uh oh, what happened?" Dad asked. "I just tailed someone to a Motel. You'll never guess who." Eddie said. "Oh boy, this should be good." Dad said. "You bet it is. Call one of those cops and send them over here right away. I found Tightass." Eddie said. "Holy shit! I will get right on it. I still have the cop's card that was on that case from the beginning. I will call him and Ted." Dad said. Eddie told Dad exactly where to send them.

Dad made the calls and went with Mr. Cray and the other officers to the Motel. The officer that was handling this case from the beginning went to the door and knocked. "Who is it?" Tightass asked. "Police, open the door or it's coming down! The officer yelled. Tightass ran to the other side of the room to try to escape through the back window. The officers broke the door down and chased after him.

They caught him outside of the window. He twisted his ankle after he jumped out. He was lying on the ground with a pathetic look on his face. The officers grabbed him, read him his rights and brought him to the car. That is where Dad was standing and smiling. Dad made sure that Tightass seen him standing there enjoying it. "Hey Mr. embezzler. I hope it paid off." Dad said as he laughed. "Screw off." Tightass said. "You know the best part? Eddie is the one that found you." Dad said as he continued to laugh. The officers took Tightass away. Mr. Cray and Dad talked for a while.

For the rest of the night Eddie avoided going back to his house. He wasn't ready for any phone calls from Billy or the girls. He spent the night at Mrs. Stages. They stayed up late and talked about what has been going on in their lives lately.

When Eddie woke up in the morning he figured he better call Billy to explain. He felt funny about what he was going to say. "Hello." Billy said as he picked the phone up. "Hey Billy, it's me Eddie. I just wanted to explain." Eddie started off. "You got some nerve.

What happened to you?" Billy asked. Eddie told Billy about the Mrs. Stages story. Billy didn't know what to say about that. He didn't know about the two of them. "Well, I would have been really mad at you, but do you know why I'm not?" Billy asked. "Why is that? Eddie asked. "Because your girl Tina helped me live out a boyhood fantasy." Billy said. "Oh man, you should be thanking me." Eddie said. "I sure am thanking you. I can't thank you enough. You know what the funny part is? She did it to get back at you for standing her up." Billy said. "Be sure to tell her that she sure showed me." Eddie joked. "Thanks again my man." Billy said. "My pleasure. I'll talk to you soon. Enjoy your new lifestyle." Eddie said as they said goodbye and hung up.

Eddie went back into bed with Mrs. Stages and held onto her and thought about how happy he is about the way everything turned out.

G. Novitsky

Chapter XV

Mom woke up early that morning. She couldn't stop thinking about Father O'Reilly and she was wondering if anything new happened with his disappearance. She decided to call the rectory to see if she could speak to Sister Taryas. "St. Peters Parish, can I help you?" The voice on the phone asked. "Good morning, my name is Julie McMullen. My son is a close friend of Father O'Reilly and I just wanted to see if there were any developments in his disappearance." Mom said. "I'm sorry, we haven't heard anything new about the situation. We are all very distraught here. We are praying for his safe return. I am sure that you and your son are doing the same." The woman said. "We sure are. Would you be able to tell me how I could get in touch with Sister Taryas?" Mom asked. There was a long pause. "Um, uh, I'm sorry but we don't perform séances at this church." The woman said. "I'm sorry? I don't know what that means." Mom said. "I certainly hope that this is not a tasteless joke. Sister Taryas passed away with three other nuns in a car accident on their way home from a retreat twelve years ago." The woman said. That must have been the same accident that the Cray's heard about.

Mom didn't know what to say. "I am very sorry. Could there be another Sister Taryas, about five foot tall, older woman, short light hair, glasses?" Mom asked. "That was her to the T. How long has it been since you have been to the church did you say?" The woman asked. "Well, um. It's been a long time since I seen her. I am sorry for the trouble." Mom said as she hung up.

"What's wrong? You don't look so good." Dad said to Mom as he walked into the kitchen. Mom explained to him how she spent twenty minutes at church the other day having a conversation with a nun who has been dead for twelve years. Dad was very confused. Mom told him the whole situation before I walked in.

Good morning Dad, good morning Mom." I said as I walked in. "Good morning Stevie." Dad said. "Stevie, do you remember at the church last week when I met Sister Taryas and I talked to her while you sat and prayed?" Mom asked. "Sure I do Mom. You told me that she said that Father O'Reilly was going to be okay." I said. "Yes, that is exactly what she told me. Stevie, do you remember what she looked like? Mom asked. "I didn't see her Mom." I replied. Mom looked around and didn't know what to say. Are you okay Mom?" I asked. "Yea, um yea, I'll be fine." Mom said.

"Do you remember your conversation with her?" Dad asked. "Yea, we spoke about Father O'Reilly and I told her about our family. She didn't say much, she nodded a lot up until we started to discuss the Parish, and then she said, oh, oh my God, do you know what she said Phil?" Mom asked. "What? What did she say Julie?" Dad asked. "She said that St. Peters is a very mysterious place." Mom said. "Wait a second, isn't that? That's what you said the woman's voice on the walkie talkie said after she sang to Stevie." Dad said. "Yes, that's why her voice sounded so familiar. Oh my God, I can't believe it." Mom said.

It took Mom quite a while to accept her discovery. She was very quiet and to herself for the rest of the day and into Monday.

Back at school David Stoub was up to his nonsense again. "Hey, did you guys hear? The freak show is back. The kidnappers must have realized what a screwball they had and threw her back." David said to the other kids at his lunch table. One or two of the kids laughed, but that seemed like it was just so David wouldn't be embarrassed by his tasteless jokes.

"Here comes the whacko now!" David said as Rachel walked into the cafeteria. She didn't hear David. Everyone looked around to see if Teddy was there. They expected another show like the last time David opened his mouth. Teddy wasn't around, but by the end of the day the word had reached him.

"Doesn't that prick learn? Didn't Jimmy McMullen just straighten his ass out for the same thing?" Teddy asked his friend Richie. "I guess he has short term memory. Do you want me to kick his ass?" Richie asked. "No, not yet. I want him to say something in front of me and I know he will. That's how stupid he is." Teddy said.

Teddy met with Jimmy after school to see what he thought about it. "I was pretty convinced that David was sincere in his apology when he spoke to me. I am surprised." Jimmy said. "I thought so too. I am not going to let this go though." Teddy said. "You shouldn't. Let me know how you're going to handle it. I'll be there for you." Jimmy said. "Thanks Jimmy. I'll keep you posted." Teddy said.

Just then another friend of Teddy's came running down the hall "David is up to it again. He is picking on another kid!" Teddy's friend said. Jimmy and Teddy headed toward where David was. On their way there they ran into Rachel. They stopped to ask her if she seen David. "We heard he was picking on someone again. We are going to end this right now." Teddy said. "I don't think you should hurt David. He is hurt enough." Rachel said as she began explaining to the guys that she overheard David's session at Gary's office. She told them that David does not have such a good life at home. She told them about David's parents being abusive to him and that convinced them to leave David alone. Luckily for David, Rachel was eavesdropping. That changed whatever would have happened to him that day.

Later on that night Billy was over at Donna's apartment. "I'm going to make a sandwich, do you want anything? Donna asked. "Yea, make me whatever you're having." Billy said. "I'm having pig ears." Donna joked. "You might as well eat them, you don't use them to listen." Billy joked back.

"Real cute smart ass. What do you want to do later on?" Donna asked. "Tell Tina to come on over and we'll have a little party." Billy said. "She doesn't have to be with us every time we get together. What is it with you and her? Do you think she is prettier than me?" Donna asked. "Oh please don't start that." Billy said. "Well, you have been talking about her a lot lately. I shouldn't have introduced you two." Donna said. "I am going out for a walk. Maybe I'll come back later." Billy said as he slammed the door behind him. He walked down the stairs and out of the main entrance to the apartment. Donna ran to her apartment door to stop him, but he was gone.

Billy lit a cigarette and started to walk. He noticed a rumbling from behind one of the bushes next to the building. He flicked his cigarette into the street and quietly walked over toward the bushes.

Billy noticed two guys crouched down speaking in another language. He stopped and watched to see what they were up to. One of the guys got up and started to pour gasoline around the ground of the building. Billy was confused for a moment. He didn't know if he should call for back up or act on his own. He figured that he wouldn't have enough time to run back upstairs to call for back up, so he ran over and grabbed the guy with the gasoline container and threw him to the ground. The other guy started to run. "Donna! Donna! Call Ted! Call Ted!" Billy started yelling as he chased the other guy across the grass.

Donna looked out of the window and seen what was going on. She quickly called the number at the precinct that Billy gave her. "Twenty seventh, can I help you?" An officer said on the other end of the line. "Yes, yes, I need Sergeant Ted Cray, quickly!" Donna said. "One moment ma' am." The officer said.

Billy caught up to the other guy and threw him to the ground. Billy started to beat him senseless as he turned around and seen the building start to go up in flames.

"Ted, those guys are here. Billy is fighting with one and the other one just set my building on fire." Donna said. "Get out of the building. We will be right over." Ted said. Ted quickly notified the fire department and grabbed Bob. They ran to the patrol car and took off.

Some other guys from the apartments helped Billy out. They managed to catch both of the guys and they tied them up. The guys tried to put the fire out with a garden hose and whatever else they could find, but the flames were just to high.

Mr. Cray and Bob pulled up with the sirens blaring and a fire truck not too far behind them. The firefighters started to put the fire out as Mr. Cray, Billy and Bob brought the guys who started the fire to the patrol car to question them. "Which one of you is Muekaz?" Mr. Cray asked. "He is not here." The taller guy said and then he quickly stopped talking. "Oh, okay, so you do know who he is." Mr. Cray said with the sound of satisfaction in his voice.

The two guys started to argue back and forth in a foreign language. "Shut up! Cut that shit out! If you got something to say, from now on it will be in English." Bob said as he gave the shorter guy a hard smack to the head.

The firemen just finished up putting the fire out and Billy ran over to Donna. "Is your apartment all right?" Billy asked. "It looks okay from out here. They said they're going to check out the inside and let us know." Donna replied. "Now we have a lead on that Muekaz guy. I am going to take a ride with Ted and Bob and see what comes of this." Billy said. "Okay, will you call me when you're finished?" Donna asked. "You bet." Billy replied. "If I'm not here, I'll be at your girlfriend Tina's." Donna said with a sarcastic tone. "Good one. Have fun, but save the real fun for when I get back." Billy said. "We may have to start without you. See you later." Donna said and they kissed each other goodnight.

First they brought the criminals back to the station and talked to them for a while. They got plenty of information from them. By the time they were ready to go for a ride to see Muekaz, the sun was coming up. Mr. Cray and Billy got into one patrol car with the criminals and Bob got into a separate car with another officer. They also had two other cars and a wagon follow them for back up.

They went by the directions of the criminals and after an hour or so they came to a broken down old house. All of the officers got out of their cars and surrounded the house. Mr. Cray, Billy and two other officers broke the door down and rushed in. The men inside the house scattered like rats.

The officers went through each room and gathered up the gang, there was a total of four men. The men were brought outside and questioned. Mr. Cray asked which one of them was Muekaz. They told Mr. Cray that Muekaz was out. One of them said that Muekaz hasn't been there for a week. The officers cuffed all of them and put them in the wagon. Two of the officers stayed in the wagon with them so not to give them a chance to make up any stories.

"Lets have a look for ourselves. These assholes are hiding something." Mr. Cray said. They searched the entire house from top to bottom. Bob and Billy were looking in the basement and they found a crawl space behind a window. Billy opened the window and shined his flashlight inside. It went back at least one hundred feet in each direction and only about two feet high from the floor to the roof. "Oh shit, this place is a mess. We have to go in. I can't see shit from here." Billy said as he crawled in deeper. He had to push boxes and broken furniture out of his way. "Bob, Bob." Billy whispered. "Yea." Bob answered. "There's someone back in that corner, I seen his eyes." Billy said. "Come back out." Bob said. "Okay, there's no one in here, lets take the ones we found and get back to the station." Billy said very loud so whoever was in there would think that he was leaving.

Bob and Billy went back to see Mr. Cray. "Ted, there is someone in the crawl space in the basement, but it is not safe to go in after him in there. It is too tight and he may have a weapon. All I seen was his eyes so I don't know exactly what we're dealing with." Billy said. "It's got to be Muekaz. Where is that crawl space from the outside?" Mr. Cray asked.

The guys went to the back of the house and Billy figured out which corner the guy was in. The crawl space was behind a beat up old deck and about a foot beneath the main floor. There was a boarded up small window that led to the crawl space. "I think it might be smarter to try and take this wall out and go in from both sides. Mr. Cray said.

They checked out the area outside and decided to contact a demolition crew to take the wall out. "This is probably going to take a while. I'm going to go to the closest precinct with the wagon and see what information I could get out of these clowns. Call me on the radio if anything happens." Mr. Cray said.

Mr. Cray and another officer sat with each of the criminals one at a time to see what information they could get out of them. They were able to find out that it was Muekaz in the basement, but he was not alone. They told Mr. Cray that Muekaz had someone else in the basement with him. Mr. Cray also found out that

Muekaz's partner usually hangs out at that house too, but he was out for the night.

Mr. Cray radioed to Bob to let him know what he found out. "So be careful, there's two guys in there. How much longer do you figure before you get through the wall?" Mr. Cray asked. "I give it about another half hour or so. Are you coming back yet?" Bob asked. "Yea, I'm just about to have these guys locked up and then I'll be back." Mr. Cray said.

When Mr. Cray arrived back at the house, the demolition crew was just finishing up and the wall was ready to come out. "You guys are quick, take fifteen for coffee." Mr. Cray said to the foreman. "Thanks officer. Do us a favor and throw away the key once you nail this son of a bitch." The foreman said. "It will be our pleasure." Mr. Cray replied.

"Don't screw around. I have a hostage in here. I'll kill him if you don't cooperate!" A voice said from inside. "What are you talking about Muekaz? You don't have a hostage." Bob said. "Yes I do and he's not going to last very long if you don't do what I say." Muekaz said. "That's how you get him to admit who he is." Bob said. "Nice job." Billy said.

"If you have someone in there, let him say something so we could believe you." Billy said. After a pause, another voice came from the basement. "Please do what he says. The Lord will work it out in his own way." The voice said. Are you satisfied now?" Muekaz asked. "Now we believe you're not alone, but who do you have with you? Is that a friend of yours?" Bob asked. "No, but he is a friend of a very nosey kid. Did you read about any missing priests in the news lately?" Muekaz asked. "That son of a bitch, he's got that priest in there." Mr. Cray said. "What are we going to do?" Bob asked.

"What are your demands?" Mr. Cray asked. "I want you to clear a path for me and the good priest to a fast car with a full tank of gas. I don't want any problems getting to the car and I don't want any problems when I drive away with the old man. If you cooperate I will call you to let you know where you could pick the old timer up. If you don't cooperate, you will be able to have what's left of him." Muekaz said.

"Okay, we will work on that. You sit tight and don't do anything stupid." Mr. Cray said. "Quite the negotiator silver tongue." Billy said with sarcasm in his voice. "Just make it fast." Muekaz replied. Mr. Cray made arrangements to have a car sent over.

After a half-hour or so, a car was delivered. Everyone cleared the way and followed Muekaz's request. Muekaz guided Father O'Reilly to the car and they drove off.

Chapter XVI

In the middle of the night, tossing and turning, I started to dream very clearly. The school bell rang and Mr. Quinn grabbed my hand and started to walk me home. After a block or two, I felt his hand slip away, that's when I found myself in front of the cemetery fence. It was extremely cold.

Mr. Stages was standing above his grave, gazing down at Tommy's head stone. Mr. Stages noticed me from the corner of his eye. He continued to look down at Tommy, but he started to talk to me. "You're a brave child. You have had to deal with more than any other child in this town has ever had to deal with. For this, I thank you. Now that my wife has someone else around the house to protect her from the fear and trauma that I need to unveil, you must tell Eddie to open the drawer. My wife wants to leave it closed in my memory, but there are some facts that need to be seen. It is the bottom drawer in the basement dresser. The key is underneath. Make sure Eddie knows to open it when Karen is not around." Mr. Stages said as he faded away.

After the dream, I woke up and wrote down the details. It took me a while to fall back to sleep. I was so anxious to talk to Eddie.

In the morning, Mr. Cray and the guys were still trying to track down Muekaz and Father O'Reilly in that car. Mr. Cray continued to question Muekaz's gang. Mr. Cray was able to get them to say where Muekaz's partner may be hiding out.

While the guys were at the station discussing their options, a letter was delivered to the station. It said:

> You kept up your end. I will keep up mine. The priest is in the back of the Ford by Lake Erie, between Monroe and Bolles Harbor.
>
> Now you can leave me alone.

Mr. Cray and the guys packed up two patrol cars and headed to that area. They brought one of the gang members, the most cooperative one. They wanted to use him to show them some of the places that Muekaz's partner hangs out.

While the guys were on their hunt, I explained my dream to Dad and he called Eddie to tell him to drop whatever he was doing and get over to our house. Mike also happened to call the house in the middle of this. I told him what was going on and he rushed over too.

Eddie got there first. Dad put on some coffee and brought him into the den. Mike pulled up a few minutes later. I explained the dream once again when everyone was together.

"We are going to have to get Karen out of the house right away." Mike said. "Let's try not to make her nervous or suspicious. I'll get Julie to ask her to lunch or something later." Dad said.

The guys arranged to have Mom call Mrs. Stages around noon to arrange plans for lunch. Eddie would be at Mrs. Stages's house waiting for the call. Once Eddie is sure that she is gone, he is going to go for the drawer. He is going to empty everything into a gym bag and then bring it back to our house so the guys could go through it. Eddie rushed over to Mrs. Stages's so their plan could begin.

Mr. Cray and the guys were getting closer to their destination. Bob was driving one car with Mr. Cray, Billy and the gangster. Three other officers from their precinct were in the other car. "This dirt bag better not be screwing with us." Billy said. "Just be careful when we pull up." Bob said. "Tell those guys to keep their distance." Mr. Cray said. Bob radioed to the car behind them to let them know to back off a little.

"That looks like the Ford." Mr. Cray said as he pointed off to the side of the road toward the water. "Yea, that's it. Exactly where they said it would be." Bob said. "Pull over here. Don't get too close just yet." Mr. Cray said.

Billy started to put on extra protective gear. He and one of the officers from the other car were the ones that were picked to approach the Ford. The other car stayed back a few yards. Mr. Cray pulled out his binoculars and canvassed the area.

Once they felt safe with the area, both squad cars pulled up on either side of the Ford. First Billy got out and crouched down on the driver's side. Then the other officer did the same on the passenger side.

Billy jumped up with his semi-automatic weapon pointed into the car. The other officer watched Billy's back. Billy noticed that there was someone tied up in the back seat. The doors were locked. He had to break the window. Billy got the door open and grabbed the man and pulled him out. It was Father O'Reilly. Billy pulled the gag from his mouth. "Bless you my son, bless you! Thank goodness you arrived. Thank goodness." Father O'Reilly said as he gasped for air.

Billy and the other officer brought Farther O'Reilly to the squad car and gave him some oxygen and water. He seemed okay, but Mr. Cray wanted to have an ambulance come for him just in case.

Father O'Reilly told the officers that Muekaz didn't beat him or anything like that. The only discomfort was being tied and gagged. Due to the position that Father O'Reilly was crammed into, he was unable to provide any information as to which direction Muekaz headed in.

When the ambulance arrived and took Father O'Reilly away, the guys began their search for Muekaz's partner. Father O'Reilly was alive, just like Sister Taryas said he would be.

Back at home, Mom called Mrs. Stages like Dad asked her to. "So, how do you feel about getting together for lunch?" Mom asked. "I don't know. Eddie just got here a little while ago and I have so much house work to get to." Mrs. Stages replied. "Oh come on, let Eddie stay and do the house work." Mom said, and Mrs. Stages started to laugh. "Honey, Julie wants me to go to lunch with her and have you do my house work." Mrs. Stages said to Eddie. "Tell her, for anyone else I would say no, but for Julie, I would love to." Eddie said as he put on Mrs. Stages's apron. "I don't know Julie." Mrs. Stages said. "Go on, I will clean up a little here and then I'll take a nap. Maybe I'll stop by to see Jerry. Go, go, go, go." Eddie said. "Oh, all right." Mrs. Stages said. "Great, I'll pick you up in twenty minutes." Mom said and they hung up.

"Julie will be here in twenty minutes, so I'm going to get ready." Mrs. Stages. said. "Twenty minutes? Wow that doesn't give you much time to get your house work done." Eddie joked.

Mr. Cray and the guys just finished checking a café that the gangster led them to, and next they were about to raid a bar where Muekaz's partner was known for hanging out. "Sometimes he sleeps upstairs from the bar. He is friendly with the owner." The gangster said. "Here goes." Billy said as he and the other officer from earlier, charged inside. "Everyone stay cool! We just want to have a look around. You! Who's upstairs?" Billy asked the bartender. "Na, na, nobody sir." The bartender said. The other officer headed up the stairs to .have a look around.

The only people in the building besides the bartender were two older fellows having drinks and watching horse racing. Mr. Cray questioned the bartender. "Whenever anyone gets too drunk to drive home, I let them sleep upstairs. That's my policy." The bartender said. "That's a damn good policy." Mr. Cray said.

Your 0 for 2 jerk off, what's next?" Billy said to the gangster. "There's another place not too far from here." The gangster said with fear and nervousness in his voice. He then led the guys to a pool hall in the next town.

Once again Billy and the other officer led the way in. There were a few guys playing pool. Billy looked around. "Holy shit! I don't believe this. I don't know whether to shake your hand or to knock you on your ass. Ted! Get in here!" Billy yelled out. Mr. Cray walked in. He looked to the corner pool table where

Billy pointed. Mr. Cray was in shock. At the corner pool table, it was none other than Vinny chalking up his pool stick.

As if Mr. Cray had forgotten about all of the trouble he had with Vinny before his disappearance, he gave Vinny a hug. Bob and Billy also walked over to greet Vinny. "I bring you here to show you Muekaz's partner and you hug him? What the hell is that all about?" The gangster asked. "This is Muekaz's partner?" Mr. Cray asked as he took a step back. "Sure is, and Muekaz is in the back." Another guy said. Mr. Cray grabbed Vinny. He held him to the ground with all of his strength. "My Daughter? My little girl? You son of a bitch! You disgusting piece of shit! I'll kill you!" Mr. Cray yelled as he punched Vinny in the face and the guys pulled him back.

Billy and the other officer charged the back room. After a scuffle and some broken glass Billy and the officer walked out with Muekaz in cuffs. "Whatever he did, I was not part of it." Vinny said. "What? If I'm going down, you're going with me." Muekaz said. "Lets straighten this out back at the station. You two are getting in separate cars." Bob said.

On the way back to the station, someone was trying to get through on the radio. There was a lot of static. Finally Mikes voice came through. "Ted? Ted? Can you hear me?" Mike asked. "Mike, Mike, is that you?" Mr. Cray asked. "Yes. I am at Phil's house with Eddie. We have some big news. I think we have the answer to the case. You have to get over here." Mike said. "We have some interesting information too. We were on our way to the station, but maybe it's better that we stop there first." Mr. Cray said.

A short while later, all of the guys were at my house. Ted, Billy and Bob went in and left Muekaz, Vinny and the other gangster in the cars being watched by the other officers.

Dad brought everyone down to the basement, where Eddie and Mike were waiting with all of Mr. Stages's secrets from his dresser drawer. "You'll never guess who is in the car." Billy said. "You'll never guess who was in the drawer." Mike said. "Vinny!" Mike and Billy said at the same time. They all looked at each other with confused looks on their faces. Billy explained how they found Vinny hanging out with Muekaz.

"That is really something. Do you want to take it a step further? Mike asked. "What's going on here?" Mr. Cray asked. "Take a look at this stuff. There are pictures in here of Vinny and Muekaz together. There is paperwork a mile high that will put the both of them away forever. All of this stuff was in Jerry's drawer at his house." Mike said. All six of them could not believe that all of the pieces were starting to come together. Going by all of the information in the drawer, they figured out that while Vinny was on the job, he was also dealing guns and drugs with Muekaz and his gang on the side.

It turned out that Mr. Stages's death was not an accident. Vinny knew that Mr. Stages had all of the information on Vinny and Muekaz. Vinny arranged to have Mr. Stages murdered by Muekaz and made it look like it was done during a drug bust. Vinny figured he had to get rid of Mr. Stages for his fear that Mr. Stages was going to contact Internal Affairs with all of the evidence.

Mr. Stages hesitated to contact Internal Affairs because Vinny was a close friend. Mr. Stages was just holding on to the evidence to use it to confront Vinny. Mr. Stages never got that opportunity.

Ted, Ted, there is a call for you on the radio." One of the officers called from outside. Mr. Cray went outside and got on the radio.

The guys in the basement were discussing ways to handle the punishment for Vinny and Muekaz. "We should kill them both right here and now." Billy said. "Death is too good for them." Mike said as he sat down. "Do you think we should see if Ted is okay out there? Remember, these guys kidnapped his Daughter?" Dad said. Once Mike got up to look outside, Mr. Cray walked back into the basement and threw Vinny to the floor. "Guess who called." Mr. Cray said. "Now what?" Eddie asked. "The precinct got the results of the autopsy from the body from the shed. It was the kid that drove the blue Camaro. Genius here was sure that it was him that hit Tommy, so he kept him locked up in that shed. Once he got the news that the schoolteacher did it he didn't know what to do, so he decided to burn the kid beyond recognition.

"You son of a bitch!" Bob said as he stood up and kicked Vinny in the ribs. "That's not all. Does this look familiar?" Mr. Cray asked as he held up a gun with a red handle and the initials K.D.L. on it. "Holy shit, that's the gun I turned in to Jerry when I found it on the street." Eddie said. "That is correct. When the other guys went through all of the shit we collected at the pool hall, they found this. It seems some scumbag of a cop stole it from the evidence area and used it in the murder of a friend of ours. The bullets found in Jerry match the bullets that this gun holds." Mr. Cray said.

"Now the question is, what are we going to do with these pieces of shit?" Mike asked. "Get them all together. We are going to lock them up for the night while I think about what we're going to do." Mr. Cray said.

The next morning Mike stopped by Mrs. Stages's to explain that her husband's murderers were found. Mrs. Stages was shocked at the outcome. "He couldn't have been a chamber maid. He had to be a cop." Mrs. Stages said. "What?" Mike asked. "Oh nothing, just something Jerry and me used to joke about. I used to ask him what he would do if he didn't become a police officer. He told me that he would take any job except being a chambermaid. He didn't have anything against maids or manual labor; he just had a strong feeling against cleaning up after people he didn't know. He said that the people you would be cleaning up after could be murderers or back stabbers and you would never know it." Mrs. Stages explained.

"Isn't that something? When we went to, uhm, uh, nevermind." Mike replied. He was about to suggest that it was Mr. Stages at Vinny's apartment the day we went there. Mike thought that it would be Mr. Stages's sense of humor to be folding towels and organizing things for a backstabbing murderer. Mrs. Stages didn't question why Mike didn't finish his sentence.

Nobody is really sure what Mr. Cray did with Vinny and Muekaz that day. The rest of the gang was locked up for weapon and drug possession along with a long list of other offences including breaking the window at O'Kelly's and setting Billy and Donna's apartments on fire.

From what I heard, it seems that a special room was opened at Murry's Inn for Vinny and Muekaz. Supposedly Mr. Cray arranged to have a hole dug under the Motel and closed off. They say that Vinny and Muekaz are chained up and unable to be heard down there. They say that once a week someone pays them a visit to feed them just so they could stay alive and continue their painful existence.

These events took place almost twenty years ago and from what I hear, those two criminals are still down there suffering. Now I am in my thirties. I am closer to Mr. Stages than I ever was when he was alive and I still talk to Tommy everyday. I learned something very important during the year after Tommy's death. I learned that they could take away your friends. They could take away your family. They could take away your possessions, but they could never take away your dreams.

About The Author

The Author was born in Brooklyn N.Y. in the early 1970's. He grew up in a suburb outside of the city. Throughout his childhood and into his adult life, his book and movie interests have been suspense with a touch of "The unknown". "Will we ever know what the other side has in store for us?" like many others, is a question that he often ponders.

Tired of stories that start off with a bang, only to leave the audience hanging, this Author decided to take his audience on a journey that will make them thankful they decided to go.

Printed in the United States
1162000002B/214-223